T0366341

Business Genetics

Business Genetics

Understanding 21st Century Corporations using xBML

Cedric G. Tyler and Stephen R. Baker

John Wiley & Sons, Ltd

Other Wiley Editorial Offices

John Wiley & Sons Inc., 111 River Street, Hoboken, NJ 07030, USA

Jossey-Bass, 989 Market Street, San Francisco, CA 94103-1741, USA

Wiley-VCH Verlag GmbH, Boschstr. 12, D-69469 Weinheim, Germany

John Wiley & Sons Australia Ltd, 42 McDougall Street, Milton, Queensland 4064, Australia

John Wiley & Sons (Asia) Pte Ltd, 2 Clementi Loop #02-01, Jin Xing Distripark, Singapore
129809

John Wiley & Sons Canada Ltd, 6045 Freemont Blvd, Mississauga, ONT, L5R 4J3, Canada

Wiley also publishes its books in a variety of electronic formats. Some content that appears in
print may not be available in electronic books.

Anniversary Logo Design: Richard J. Pacifico

British Library Cataloguing in Publication Data

A catalogue record for this book is available from the British Library

ISBN 978-0-470-06654-6 (HB)

Typeset in 11/16pt Trump Medieval by SNP Best-set Typesetter Ltd, Hong Kong

Contents

Acknowledgements

THE AUTHORS WISH TO THANK, FIRST AND FOREMOST, the 1000-plus xBML Business Geneticists in the industry. These are the folk who have taken concept to reality and are making a difference every day in the workplace. It is through your toil and tribulation that we are able to understand, define, improve and catapult (sometimes kicking and screaming!) our corporations into the 21st century. Your efforts have enabled us to get the necessary industry recognition to help make the invaluable work you are doing more recognizable by leadership and industry experts. We also acknowledge the sometimes super-human efforts of the folks at BusinessGenetics and xBML Innovations. You all have forged a new path in the industry and have truly 'made a difference'. Again, without your stellar efforts this book would still be a pipedream. A special thanks to Hannah, Catherine and Donna for your assistance in editing and critiquing this book. The authors also thank their families and friends who have recognized that 'something special' is afoot, and have allowed us the space to indulge our passions. It is not easy, especially for Donna and Linda, to live and support two passionate extremists that genuinely want to change the world!

Thanks, again, to you all!

Cedric and Steve

Preface

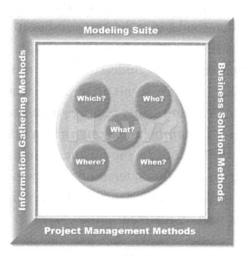

THE CONTINUED HIGH PRODUCTION OUTPUT OF MANY corporations is at risk. Over past decades, we have made significant inroads to improve productivity. Information technology advances, particularly the Internet, have been significant contributors. Additionally, we have seen important contributions in supply-chain management, manufacturing techniques and a workforce that is becoming ever more skilled. But to cope with the *massive business complexity of 21st century commerce*, we require *a new way of thinking* about and describing how corporations function. We need to understand this foundationally, like never before. We must begin to understand the genetic code or makeup of the corporation. We also need to ensure that everyone in the business is able to comprehend this new world of massive *corporate complexity*, understanding explicitly their role and their associated corporate contribution.

A new 'business-oriented' method (or language) for understanding the organization's genetic code must be established, one that is understood top to bottom, across functional silos and those on both sides of the Enterprise Divide.[1] For massive business complexity to be understood, we must be able to state this genetic code in terms that those who must work within it can understand – this requires a **business definition** that is *precise and unambiguous*, one that is *understood and meaningful* to all factions in the business community. Until corporations learn to truly understand the business, and communicate that understanding, fewer and fewer significant productivity gains will be realized.

To address these complex challenges, we will introduce a flexible 'technology' which will show you how to map out the organization's genetic code and *define complex (or simple!) business*, like never before. We will show you how to truly *leverage the business definition*, and directly equate the result to *quantifiable ROI* (i.e. income statement improvement). We will show you how to finally get the business to truly engage in the definition of the business and the use of these definitions. And lastly, we will show you how to do all of this in a *fraction of the time of traditional approaches*.

---

[1] The enterprise divide is used to describe the (significant) disconnect or gap between 'the business' and Information Technologists.

We also spawn an entire *new era of business definition, planning and improvement at all levels of the organization* (operational, tactical and strategic). We will introduce the notion of a (true) **'business model'** or **genetic blueprint.** We will have the capability to truly understand the genetic makeup of our organizations. Or stated in other terms, we will enter the realm of **Business Genetics.**

The eXtended Business Modeling Language™ (xBML™) is such a business definition 'language'.[2] It is the science of mapping out corporate genes. xBML doesn't *look* like a language at all. Unlike most languages, which consist of words and sentences and paragraphs, xBML is a *graphical language*. It is a language made up of diagrams, with each element within the diagrams having a formally defined meaning. This, then, is similar in concept to the DNA structures biologist use to map out human genes. In a sense, each element in a diagram is similar to a word, with the diagram forming sentences. A group of diagrams is analogous to a paragraph, and when all the diagrams are combined, you have the graphical equivalent of a genetic map – and one that captures a synoptic representation of part or all of a business.

These intuitive diagrams or genetic maps simply *make sense* to everyone. Executives can state their vision and goals in xBML terms and operational units can *actually understand and implement* them, using the same language. Likewise, managers and other personnel in organizational units (e.g. IT,

---

[2] 'xBML' is a registered trademark of BusinessGenetics, Inc.

Sales, etc.) can, for the first time, *clearly articulate and unambiguously communicate* organizational needs in a common language. xBML bridges the enterprise divide, providing the means for clear and concise 'business-centric' communications between everyone in the organization, including business and IT.

Providing a means for clear, unambiguous corporate communication and understanding is important enough but xBML is also a powerful 'front end' to virtually *every* corporate initiative.

What we mean by 'front end' is that if you examine all the initiatives (projects) underway in today's corporations and organizations what you will discover is the 'first task' in many of these is to 'understand' and 'document' the business/ organization.

The resultant models or genetic maps can be used as the starting point or foundation for initiatives ranging from Business Process Management (BPM) to Business Improvement, Regulatory Compliance, Business Requirements, Information Technology deployment, Mergers and Acquisitions, to name a few.

Deploying a method to *accurately and completely describe the business, once, and then relentlessly reuse this output* is no longer a desired notion but a reality, and will become a *competitive necessity*. Some Fortune 500 corporations in the USA have already realized significant gains from the approach outlined in this book and are positioning to be the commercial leaders of the 21st century.

The book advocates the prolific use of xBML as the new global standard for business definition, in order to ignite a new discipline of business modeling. It introduces the notion of a more scientific methodology to map out the genetic code of corporations, thereby allowing us to explicitly understand corporations, and more importantly, enable us to tinker with these genetic building blocks, to build sustainable and healthy 21st-century corporations.

We will show you a technology that started not in the boardroom of a mega-corporation or in academia or in the theoretical musings of an industry analyst, but evolved over many years and earned success the hard way – at the corporate grassroots level, entirely 'under the radar screen'. And, most importantly, we will attempt to convince you that this is *fundamentally important to you and your corporation.*

Thousands have already been trained in the methodology and the ground swell is happening. *Indeed a brave new world of commerce is dawning and those equipped with the right 21st-century tools for facing this enormous challenge will reap the just rewards.*

1

What's the issue and why should I care?

WHY SHOULD YOU BOTHER TO PAY ATTENTION? Frankly, the last thing corporate leaders need is yet another fad. Another low-yielding, resource-consuming monster that we have to do simply because it's the new, new thing.

Well, regardless of new trends and industry fads, the real issue is the inescapable fact that conducting business in the 21st century is becoming more and more complex. Everyone in the corporation is grappling with an ever-increasing, complex choreography of dynamics within the corporation – dynamics that we may, or may not, even be conscious of. Some of these dynamics are internal to the corporation and many are external dynamics. So what are the *primary dynamics* that influence business complexity?

1. Enormous market complexity
   (a) Globalization
   (b) Increasing substitutes
   (c) Hyper-competition

(d) Increasing new entrants (especially from developing economies)

(e) Product and service convergence

(f) Consolidation

(g) New and disruptive technologies.

2. Organization complexity
   (a) Virtual organizations
   (b) Multiple mergers and acquisitions
   (c) Multiculturalism
   (d) Outsourcing
   (e) Consensus management
   (f) Aging workforce
   (g) Non-institutionalized corporate knowledge
   (h) Generation next values
   (i) Corporate improvement initiatives.

3. Regulations and compliance

– and oh so many, many more. . . .

Unfortunately, there are just so darn many, so let's abstract most of these complexity contributors or drivers into one category of singular importance. Let's lump these drivers together under the label of conducting business in the 21st century or **21st-century commerce (21CC).**

One of the premier thought leaders and an expert in systems thinking, Peter Senge, has some interesting observations about complexity:

three types of increasing complexity are at the root of organizations' and societies' toughest problems:

1) dynamic complexity: cause and effect distant in time and space

2) social complexity: diverse stakeholders with different agendas and worldviews

3) generative complexity: emergent realities wherein solutions from the past no longer fit.

In the face of such complexity, the very concept of 'problem solving' can be an impediment. It can lead us to think of fixing something that is broken. It can lead to imposing solutions from the past. And, it can lead to seeing reality as the adversary rather than the ally.

But let's think about complexity for a second. We all agree that business is more complex, yet if we do a review of the literature it's difficult, if not impossible, to find common agreement as to what complexity means. For the purposes of this book we are going to define complexity in the following way: there are more things to do, more people/organizations/systems doing them, more places in which they occur (regional/national/international), more time constraints involved in their performance and probably the biggest contributor to complexity is that there is more information, or at least more data.

So we agree business is getting more and more complex, and this is perfectly in line with the thoughts of academics, industry analysts and thought leaders of the day. All agree that commerce is getting ever more complex.

All agree too that we should build **business-driven processes,** rather than exist in **process-driven businesses**. All agree that corporate stovepipes must go, and rapidly be replaced with nimble, customer-focused business processes that are readily automated. All agree that we urgently need to address these significant challenges. And all agree that corporations which fail to adapt to the emerging complexity will be severely and negatively impacted.

Few agree on how to face and address these 21CC challenges. Indeed, many have not even thought much of the *tools required* for 21CC. Many naively assume that the tools are already in place. Many are in for a nasty surprise!

Another major reason (and arguably the most important reason for caring about the content of this book) is, like it or not, our organizations spend a great deal of time, energy and resources attempting to understand and describe themselves.

What we mean by this, is that every corporate change and improvement initiative spends 10 to 50 (or more) percent of its effort attempting to understand and describe the business. In fact the first step in every Six Sigma, Lean, organizational improvement, BPM, SOX, and all the other multitude of initiatives is to (you guessed it) *understand and describe* the business.

We conservatively estimate, that 5 to 10 percent of our corporate expenses are consumed trying to understand and describe the business. In a multi-trillion dollar economy that's a lot of beans.

If we could gain just a small modicum of efficiency in this endeavor the savings would be astronomical.

If your organization is not a victim of complexity and you have no corporate change initiatives or projects, then no need to read further. But for everyone else the simple challenge is: **how on earth are you *going to understand your business and what do you truly have at your disposal to help?***

We believe Business Genetics *will provide a significant part of the answer.*

2

Why are tools to understand business so inadequate?

THE WAY WE DESCRIBE AND PLAN BUSINESS IS foundationally flawed. Our current practices, methods and tools, techniques and technology are still in the Dark Age, or at least the last century. The industry abounds with 'junk science' approaches, instantiated with archaic software tools that relentlessly compound the problem and detract from meaningful gains in productivity.

Adam Smith, of course, has served us well. The notion of the Division of Labor in a low-technology era has been nothing short of foundational in terms of its impact on commerce. Specialization of the workforce and the creation of 'divisional stovepipes' is a concept that is firmly entrenched in most corporations today. Indeed the notion makes tons of sense, in pre-21CC.

However, the times they have indeed changed. We are no longer dealing with a semi-literate workforce, with a high concentration of 'simple' manufacturing. Commerce has changed fundamentally. It has changed irrevocably. And it has embraced marvelously complex technology and systems. It is staffed with armies of technology savvy and well-educated knowledge workers. Besides, organizing our corporations in this fashion does little to held us truly understand how the corporation functions.

Crudely put, a heck of *a lot has changed*. So, besides the division of labor concept, what approaches do we have to better understand our corporations?

Well, the pervasive flowcharts of today are, in large part, based on theory by Taylor and Gilbreth developed over 100 years ago . . . and in the succeeding century no foundational improvement or change has been made to the way we describe business!

There have been a few notable attempts to introduce and standardize business definition (modeling) notation. One of these was IDEF (ICAM Definition Language) invented and developed in the 1970s and 1980s. This was an attempt, funded by the US Air Force, to produce a vendor-independent SADT-based modeling language. Others were Object Orientation (OO) and, more recently, BPMN (Business Process Modeling Notation). These suffer from being too technical and only focused on specific or limited uses – most often some sort of automation or IT-based effort. They were all introduced for a specific intent and have largely been embellished by well-meaning practitioners, far beyond their original intent.

The simple fact is that we are now firmly entrenched in the 21st century and the best 'science' provided to us to describe business consists of Microsoft® Word® based business planning templates, Microsoft® Excel® spreadsheets (measuring hypothetical income and resource consumption, which is ill-defined at best) and a hodgepodge (720 at the last count!) of disjointed and *very artistic* 'process mapping' software tools/techniques (e.g. the most prevalent of all, Microsoft® Visio® or Microsoft® PowerPoint®).

In other words, we are seriously ill-equipped to better understand, improve and manage the behemoth corporations of the 21st century and their **massive complexity**. There is little doubt that the tools of the trade are severely lacking.

These tools may have served us somewhat adequately for 20th-century commerce, but a fresh perspective and a new wave of 'disruptive' technology is desperately needed to guide managers, business professionals and leadership into the era of global, hyper-competitive and very complex 21CC.

This book will do exactly that. That is, we will show you why current thinking and approaches for defining business are *severely* deficient, flawed and frankly dated. We will present an entirely new way of thinking about, looking at and defining business. This new way of understanding business complexity has the potential to reap enormous productivity gains and position corporations for 21CC.

The approach described in this book is not wishful thinking or academic postulation. The concepts, methods and techniques have been practically applied in approximately 30 of the Fortune© 500 corporations, as well as many federal agencies, with often astonishing results. It has been an arduous struggle to invent, innovate, define, refine and practically deploy *a way of thinking that can play an instrumental role in reshaping 21st century corporations.*

2.1   How did we get here?

Simply stated, we got where we are by taking techniques and tools created in a simpler time and attempting to adapt them to understand the genetic makeup of the 21st century corporation.

The thought leaders and software vendors of our time have done a wonderful job of motivating us to improve business: Total Quality Management, ERP, CRM, KM, Workflow, Business Process (Re)engineering (BPR), yet more (beyond) BPR, Six Sigma sect (sometimes more like cult) and now Business Process (or Performance) Management (or Monitoring) (BPM). Even the gurus are still a tad confused on this one! In fact, if ever we saw a title waiting for content, this would be it! All of these software offerings are advocated as the panacea to our business efficiency, accuracy and effectiveness ills.

The common denominator here is that *all* of the above *assume* (and we all know how dangerous assumptions can be) that business can be depicted using artistic and unstructured 'junk science' – essentially a (somewhat random) temporal string of activities linked together.

In fact, it's worse than that. Most practitioners intentionally 'dumb down' the schematic definitions of the business, or worse yet, resort to text, 'pictograms', PowerPoint® slides and even spreadsheets!

This is analogous to a doctor attempting to understand the explicit nature of an injured knee by feeling it with his hands rather than using an MRI. Or, an auto mechanic attempting to diagnose a 2007 automobile's problems by listening to it rather than connecting it to a diagnostic computer.

These grossly oversimplified representations rather defeat the purpose of describing (and fixing) business complexity in the first place. Why do they dumb it down? Because they don't have the language or the tools to talk about business in a way that will make sense to everyone. They have no framework for creating business definitions. The resulting definitions are a hodgepodge of subjective information compiled by multiple individuals who have most likely biased the descriptions with their own personal experience.

The simple truth is: **If you can't describe it, you can't fix it!**

And certainly, if you describe it poorly, your fix will be poor.

To illustrate the variety, inconsistency and incomprehensibility of current 'process modeling' (business definition) practices, we have collected the examples in Figures 2.1–2.4. All, real-life extracts from Fortune 500 companies. (Our personal favorite is the 'pictogram' in Figure 2.2, that surely cannot depict any meaningful business knowledge.)

But wait, I sense dissension in the ranks! I hear the backroom boys saying: 'Of course there are more robust ways of representing business (and its associated complexity).'

Well, yes. A case in point is Figure 2.3. Oh my gosh, is this for real? Such a concoction (which is usually spawned from mostly defunct Information System/Science methodologies)

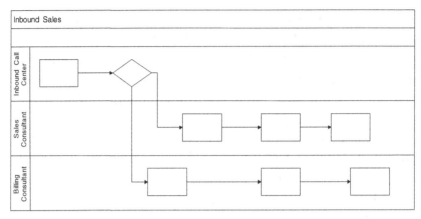

Figure 2.1 Simple two-dimensional process chart.

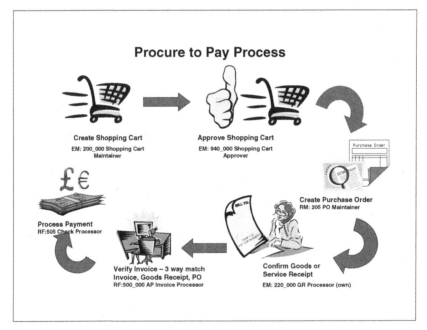

Figure 2.2 Pictogram process chart.

have as much chance of success as a simple, intuitive way to describe business as Idi Amin had of winning the Nobel Peace Prize. Today's business professionals should not tolerate such techno-trash.

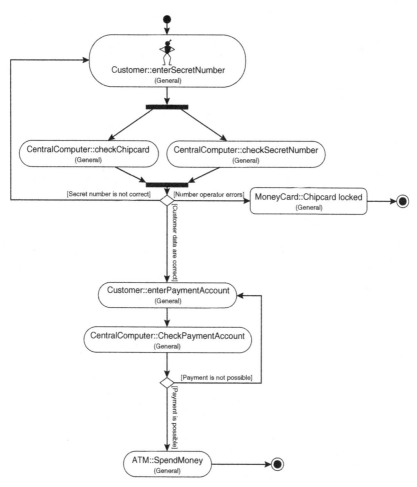

Figure 2.3 Object-oriented process flow.

How did we develop such rudimentary and even naive techniques for depicting our business? One issue is that many of the self-proclaimed process gurus told us to look at the business monoscopically, by addressing *only the activities* (and inputs/outputs, whatever they are). The result is business process definitions at an almost juvenile level.

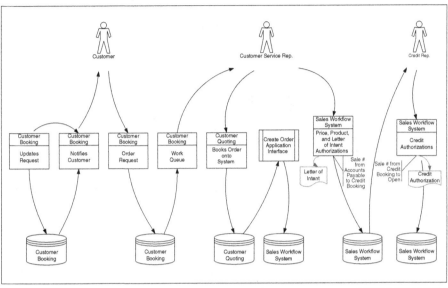

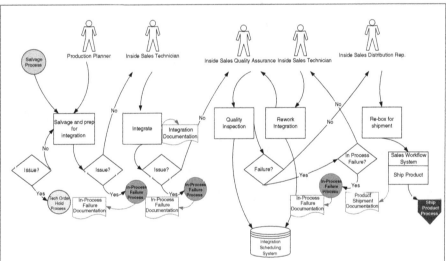

Figure 2.4 Two-dimensional process charts from global consulting firm.

Box 2.1   Hot off the press – from a $9 billion Fortune 500 company

Model: representation of Order-to-ship process (one of 44 similar models)

Method used to create models: Heaven only knows!

Authors: 'Final few' consulting company (Process 'experts')

Estimated cost (for all 44 models): $1.25 million

Estimated hours spent interviewing business: 2112

Estimated cost of business participation: $116160

Estimated shelf life of models: 6–12 weeks

Estimated ROI: Are you kidding!

The above serves to illustrate by means of a real-life example how an enormous amount of resource can be expended by a major consulting firm only to deliver marginal value.

2.2   Business definition à la 20th century

The *repetitive* downfall of all of the historic business definition/depiction approaches and theory is the fact that they neglect to think about *what* we are describing in the first place. In fact, ask almost anyone to define the **components of a business** (or to define an organization) and you will get as many answers as folk you ask the question of. Many will reference various 'artifacts', for example, organization charts, 'process' maps from (pick your favorite large ERP vendor or consulting company), systems flowcharts, spreadsheets, etc. Or, oftentimes you will get the chronically vague reference to 'People, process and technology'. Textbook mumbo-jumbo at its finest!

The fact is no one really knows! Unlike other disciplines (let's all pause and reflect on this word[1]), management/business theory lacks a universally agreed (or even defined) *foundation or framework* upon which we describe business. Please take another moment and compare this notion of a lack of formal business definition theory (i.e. what does business really consist of?) to almost any other discipline, including:

1. *Journalism*: the *Who, What, Where, When?* story framework

2. *Nuclear engineering*: the Rutherford and Bohr atomic models

3. *Building science*/architecture, engineering (mechanical, electrical, plumbing): isometric drawing

---

[1]Discipline is any training intended to produce a specific character or pattern of behavior, especially training that produces moral, physical, or mental development in a particular direction. Discipline, while often thought to be a coercive mechanism, can be a collaborative process of building consensus regarding accepted behavior within institutions and society. (http://www.Wikipedia.com).

4. *Biology*: Linnaean system of classification of organisms

5. *Electrical engineering*: electronic circuit design, Cauchy–
   Riemann equations, Fourier and Laplace Transform theory,
   Z Transform.

The fact is we (academics, business leaders, business profes-
sionals, consultants, industry analysts, etc.) really don't have
a sound understanding of the theoretical/foundational com-
ponents of business.

So, just imagine that we constantly 'tinker' with the business (usually isolated pieces like the organization structure,
task assignments, application systems, responsibilities, etc.)
without understanding all the pieces and how they interre-
late! Surely a recipe with potentially disastrous, or certainly
less than desirable, consequences!

In defining and improving or even automating complex business, many adopt a 'trust us' philosophy, implying that there
is some underlying 'professional' approach or even methodology. Nothing is usually farther from the truth. We guarantee
that if you ask simple questions like: How would you define
a business *process*? or What theory do you use to ensure consistent business definitions?, in most instances, the question
will not even be understood! Yes, that's how bad the industry
is. It's an unfortunate reality.

Of course, admitting this (especially should you push on this
issue) you will, without doubt, experience fierce resistance
and most will revert to the 'flat earth' argument that you
should trust them since they do this every day for a living.
So, when you hear these 'defensive' positions, consider what
Lex Mckee says:

Ridicule is normally the immediate response – 'The Earth is round? Don't be ridiculous!' followed by aggressive denial or suppression of the idea. When, however, sufficient people buy into a new idea, then all of a sudden it becomes accepted as the new norm. It is as if the collective brain has built a new 'path of least resistance' to an idea and it becomes habit.

Or:

John Locke

New opinions are always suspected, and usually opposed, without any other reason but because they are not already common.

But back to the point.

Please pause and think about this topic for a moment. We don't know what a business consists of, but we are going to solve our business issues. Hm ... (*Remember, if you can't describe it, you can't fix it!*)

And even if we look at the pundit's definitions of business (process) depiction, we see room for evolving these definitions in light of 21CC. For example, the well-known and very successful Champy and Hammer definition of business 'process' (the core 'backbone' of business) is defined as: *a collection of activities that takes one or more kinds of inputs and creates an output that is of value to a customer.*

In today's massively complex business world, this definition is about as insightful as saying: 'an airplane consists of a number of components that collectively provide value to the passenger.' That is, it provides a (very) good context for a business definition (process) but really does not elucidate what the process consists of. This may give insights into the behavior of organizations, particularly those entrenched in functional silos. The techniques used to describe the process were treated as somewhat of a 'black box' and left largely to the devices of the process modeler. However, the Business Re-engineering focus was to encourage business-driven processes and erode eons of organization function-centered thinking. All goodness.

But in today's massively complex world we must have a more powerful and insightful definition of our business. The 'black box' must be understood. We simply must comprehend the inner workings of the business (process), at a detailed level. We must be able to map out the business as we map out human DNA. Only then can we truly understand what makes the corporation tick.

Further, these somewhat vague and usually high-level definitions will 'break down' if used to try and understand even relatively simple business processes. You will find that it is difficult even to reach consensus on the start or end (i.e. scope or range) of the 'process'. Equally perplexing is how to gather the 'collection' of activities *and* the major issue of grouping unequal activities (different activity *levels*) together. And we do this *randomly*? Until it *feels* right? Or until the business representatives simply 'give up' and capitulate, so that they can go back to doing their 'real work'!

Now imagine trying to define a Quote to Order 'process' in a $13 bn telecommunications company with three major lines of business, over 1000 products and services, with thousands of business folk in a national geography! Good luck!

Academics also appear to be blissfully unaware of both the scale and magnitude of this issue and certainly unaware of the enormous leaps in productivity that are entirely feasible. Of course, there have been very insightful 'academic' contributions – mainly quadrants and market force models – which have greatly aided in understanding the complex forces that our corporations must contend with. Very insightful, to say the least – but, again, these are big and high-level contributions.

We need more to understand the essential workings of the corporation at the detailed level. We must have a consistent, repeatable 'genetic blueprint' of how the business operates. And in this domain there is little theory to guide us. Even many industry analysts appear to advocate that the issue of business complexity can be 'bought away' by advocating (mostly) complex (BPM, ERP and many other) software solutions.

At the risk of being too forward, only the mother of all morons would attempt to solve the enormous challenges by purchasing current business process automation software and installing it without an explicit business understanding. Having still not learned from the 20th-century attempts to 'buy our business problems away', the industry is now hot and heavy to acquire BPM and SOA (service-oriented architecture) software. Right, that will solve the problem!

Please stop and think about this for a moment. Business is so massively complex, we will grasp at any software tool alleging that it can automate new business (processes).

Well, it turns out that a 'fool with a tool' is usually a bigger fool!

Garbage in, garbage out! How can we automate something we can't even define?

One more time for heaven's sake: **if you can't describe it, you can't improve or automate it (the business)**. An undeniable truism.

And expanding this truism further: **the better (more detailed/ accurate, etc.) you describe it (the business), the better the improvement or automation result**. And another important fact is: **If you describe it (the business) *poorly,* your improvements or automation results will be *poor.***

Yes, the notion of automated process is exceedingly tempting but please look at how most, if not all of these 'bells and whistles' software tools define 'the business (process)'. You guessed it, unstructured (no rules) boxes and arrows. We have seen many instances of clients shelving pretty sophisticated (and very expensive) software because the underlying business definitions are so naive that they border on the ludicrous.

If they are implemented, and you examine the situation in detail, the organization treats the new software like the body reacts to a splinter. What we mean is, if you look closely you'll discover that the new software has been encapsulated by a new set of manual processes. In some cases these new processes are supported by Access databases, Excel spreadsheets and new forms and reports. What is most concerning is that the primary purpose of these new processes is to convert the information the business needs to operate, into a form consumable by the new software product and likewise, convert the information contained in new software product to a form that is valuable to the operations of the business. We have seen this construct in many of the Fortune companies we have observed over the course of the last two decades.

What a gigantic waste (again). And how unfortunate. If we did have robust, formal (rule-based), complete and detailed business representations, our software tools (no matter the 'flavor de jour') have more than some promise. BPM/SOA vendors, like many others, have made the vain assumption that we all know how to define a business (process), just as Microsoft® did when it launched BizTalk® – enough said.

Lastly, some of our friends in IT have attempted to solve the problem of defining/describing business by means of 'techno'-centric mumbo-jumbo. Methods that may be, and indeed are, very useful to define and build application systems usually **do not**, we repeat do not, make much sense in defining business.

A case in point is the 'object-oriented' (OO) world, where techno-centric leaders have assumed (here we go again, to quote a famous US President!) what's good for the goose is good for the gander. In fact an entire slew of (limited-value) software tools to define/depict business has been thrust upon the business via the IT budget. In fairness, this is certainly better than nothing, you know, 'the whole one eye is better in the land of the blind'. So the motivation is truly admirable.

Our personal advice: throw that nonsense out (of the business) as soon as you can!

This OO theory (from a business definition perspective) is based on the theory that the world consists of natural 'objects', which are conveniently defined as 'nouns' (pick a noun, *any* noun). We need go no further. The principal challenge here is trying to conduct a business definition work session with business SMEs (subject matter experts) in any complex corporation and asking them to describe all the nouns (objects) that exist in, let's say, the supply chain. *Go on, we double-dare you!*

Lastly, many software vendors and management consulting firms appear to be trapped in a quagmire of unoriginal thought. The major focus has been on applying 'back end' analytical methods, tools and techniques to 'fix' business (process) problems. Absolutely, some of these methods and techniques warrant serious considerations and good science abounds (for example, in Six Sigma, Lean, etc.). But the major issue here is: *garbage in, garbage out!* That is, the 'thing' that most of these folk measure (now very prevalent in the new, new thing – i.e. BPM/SOA) is a pile of meaningless manure. Or, according to the 'proper' definition, a 'random' string of activities. Yeah, go analyze that!

2.3 But we have had some (limited) success

Yes, we certainly have. But based on countless interactions with innumerable Fortune 500 companies, we find that business is often so 'broken' that sitting in a conference room, holding hands and singing 'Kumbaya', while focusing on the business 'process' at hand, would probably yield a somewhat successful result.

Let's talk about Six Sigma and Lean for a moment. These two currents (or tidal waves) have done a great deal to bring process improvement to the masses. They have done so by repackaging and 'cook booking' existing statistical techniques and typing project success to financial results. This has allowed far more of the organization to be involved and committed to process improvement than previously attempted quality approaches. However, they have contributed no value in advancing the science or discipline of understanding and describing process in a consistent and repeatable manner. The process understanding used in Six Sigma is based entirely on the classic flowchart of the past. This is understandable as the roots of these initiatives are process engineering from a manufacturing environment.

The dilemma is, that once you have harvested the so-called low-hanging fruit (which has become more and more scarce), how do you deal with the massively complex and intricate business issues? Let alone deal with the challenge of 'fixing' business issues 'up- or downstream' and inadvertently, and worse still, unknowingly causing equal or bigger issues in up-/downstream business areas/processes! (But we guess this does create an ongoing demand for improvement projects!)

So, this book was written as a consequence of the shortcomings of 20th-century approaches to recognize two simple premises:

1. We lack a sound 'theoretical' framework to help us understand what business truly consists of inside the 'black box'.

2. We simply do not have adequate methods and tools to describe how complex 21CC operates.

A final thought here: if you are still unconvinced as to the inadequacy of our business definition and depiction theory, method and tools, and have perhaps even experienced a modicum of success in 'welching' out some meaningful Six Sigma improvement, then please ask yourself the question: *what methods/tools/approaches do you have in your enterprise to define enormously complex business?* And can we describe business in a *detailed, consistent, repeatable and rigorous manner* that will enable stakeholders to truly understand the business?

We are sure that if you truthfully answer the question, you will discover, at best, a plethora of informal and largely 'artistic' 20th-century approaches to define/describe business (flowcharts, process maps, Visio® diagrams, IDEF charts, etc.) and most probably a small band of very, very smart 'Business analyst (non-replicable) Heroes'. More probably, the answer will be that you possess one (or more) drawing tools – no, please don't confuse these free-format diagram editors or drawing tools, with a rule-based methodology, based on a foundational **business definition** theory.

We would argue that we are consequently and most probably ill-equipped to deal with what the 21st century has already introduced; *massive complexity (regardless of the other factors we discussed earlier).*

Consider a nuclear refueling outage example – a 'process' that consists of *over 10 000 activities*, involves *hundreds of different skill sets*, has a *multi-million dollar daily direct impact* to the income statement and requires an *intricate choreography*, and a myriad of challenges, including:

- Aging/aged workforce

- A daunting assortment of regulations and safety controls

- Poorly defined process

- Below industry median performance record

- A myriad of contractors, subcontractors and even sub-subcontractors, etc.

How would you even start to define such massive complexity? How would you make sense of all these intertwined factors? What tools would you use to help understand the operation?

A daunting challenge and very pertinent questions indeed. Clearly, 20th-century management science and business depiction technology will only deliver a partial answer. Clearly much more is needed to meet the challenge.

Confronted with this set of new challenges, it is clear that we should warmly embrace any effort to advance management science, in the realm of business understanding.

We sincerely hope that, in this chapter, we have convinced you that you really should care about better understanding how your business operates, and (to put it in our terms) explicitly describing the corporate DNA.

Industry desperately needs new thoughts, methods, management science and tools to help cope with the massive complexity of 21CC.

3

OK (enough already), so What must be done?

I keep six honest serving-men
(They taught me all I knew);
Their names are What and Why and When
And How and Where and Who.

(Rudyard Kipling, *The Elephant's Child*)
Reproduced by permission of AP Watt.

By now, we hope you agree that we need a new generation of **management 'tools'** to better understand business complexity, increase production and map out our corporate genes.

We need to start by going back to the proverbial drawing board and ask ourselves what on earth are we trying to define/depict when we try and represent the complexities of business? In all of the thousands of years past, what essentially does a business or organization *consist of*?

Just like other disciplines, such as Biology, Physics, Engineering, etc., *we need to better understand the very fabric, core or foundational elements of a business or organization.*

Will we ever move beyond high-level abstractions like 'People, process and technology', or 'a sequence of activities'?

Can we more accurately define the **theoretical foundation** of all organizations? Can we define its actual genetic makeup or DNA?

Yes, we can, and indeed must! Other disciplines have done this and made major strides forward.

For example, the world of physics quite literally took a quantum leap forward by fundamentally rethinking the atomic model. For decades, the early Rutherford and Bohr model (nucleus with orbiting electrons) served us well. It tied in very nicely with the mechanical world of Newtonian physics (and then current perspectives of the world). Prompted by unexplained phenomena and anomalies in the natural world, theorists like Einstein, Oppenheimer, Bohr, Planck, Schrodinger *et al.*, *went back to basics* and quite literally **redefined reality** with quantum physics, resulting in a **new world** of incredible *technological advances.*[1]

---

[1]Quantum theory has enabled such technologies as satellites, space exploration, magnetic levitation, LED technology, lasers, cell phones, weapons, super computing, etc.

Similarly, physicians can only accomplish the modern marvels of medicine as a direct understanding of the systemic decomposition of the human body. In fact it takes many years to gain this understanding but the results of having this knowledge enable the treatment of diseases that were fatal.

Oftentimes, *rethinking the fundamentals and our time-tested notions* can be highly beneficial indeed. Rethinking time-tested and 'comfortable' notions are never easy – just ask Tony Buzan. We speak from first-hand experience. We have introduced the 'disruptive' notions in this book to very many 'process' experts, 'Final Four' consultants, managers, etc.

The reaction is almost always quite predictable when raising 'foundational' questions such as: What are you trying to describe? What does a process (or business) consist of? What rules do you use to describe/depict a business/process? What exactly do you place inside the 'box' on the process map?, etc. The question posed usually solicits an initial ominous silence, followed by (visible) skepticism, (extreme) defensiveness and even indignation!

It seems we are challenging the all too comfortable and secure world of many career professionals, and even reputable con-sulting organizations, by asking these foundational questions. The ramifications are rather scary for many of these folk!

Essentially many careers and billions of dollars of revenue are at risk if they admit to this new way of thinking! It is far easier and convenient to 'wish' these new notions away than to embrace them and advance 21CC.

Then there are the few who are not threatened and are, in fact, genuinely excited. These are the *visionaries* who perceive the immense potential, the possibilities and the rewards that lie ahead. Yes, they are often the corporate 'mavericks' and are sometimes found in the most unlikely of places, in finance or sales or engineering, etc. These visionaries make it all worthwhile. They are the **change agents** of the future. These few will enable us to boldly embrace new ideas and technologies to drive the wheels of commerce in the 21st century.

As previously discussed, in the case of rethinking business science and theory (un)fortunately given what actually exists, *there is not a whole lot to rethink* (especially in comparison to the world of physics). So, if we really, truly think about this long and hard (over two decades, in our case), the answer is in fact (deceptively) simple.

After struggling with these 'foundational questions' for many years and drawing upon theory and (applied) research from many sources, we have concluded that any, and indeed every business (in any industry sector) foundationally (and always) consists of *five – **and only five** – **things***.

These 'things' we will call **dimensions** and if we can understand them and (even better) represent them graphically (because the human mind best deals with pictures), and if they are defined with some amount of rigor or science, then this is akin to discovering the very foundational 'atomic' or 'genetic' building blocks of the organization. In other words, we have 'discovered' the essence of the organization, the very atoms or elements that make up its very DNA! And, if we have discovered these 'atomic' foundations or business genetic building blocks, we will have insights and understanding of the business as never before.

We can also do some amazing things once we can define/ depict business in five dimensions: for example, really understand what's going on, fix broken business, automate business, root out *unproductive business practices and leverage* these new *business representations* across the entire enterprise, for a multitude of uses. Further, we can literally understand the very corporate 'genome', and *reuse these definitions* (let's call them **business models**) to identify and fix broken business genes.

As we said earlier, if we can do this, the gains will be nothing short of quantum.

All right, so what are the five foundational dimensions of any organization? Well, simply stated, we have discovered that to understand any (and indeed *every*) organization we simply must know the following:

1. work activities (we do work, we performs actions)

2. at a place

3. by someone or some group

4. at a specific point in time

5. using and creating information (an absolute necessity to perform the work above).

All of which exist to accomplish *a specific, defined purpose.*

So, simply stated, if we isolate the *dimensions* of any organization, we can better *understand* this **conglomerated complexity**, or *how* a business operates by simply 'breaking the business up' into the above five simple dimensions, namely:

1. **What** work is performed?

2. **Where** do we do work?

3. **Who** does work?

4. **When** is work done?

5. **Which** information is needed to do work?

Or depict it in a simple graphic (Figure 3.1).

Also, we have discovered that all of the above dimensions *only exist* to **enable a given, defined purpose** *(Why?)* to be accom-

Figure 3.1 The xBML framework.

plished. (Note that if any of the above do not directly support a stated business purpose, either the purpose is incorrect *or* the dimension is redundant – i.e. does not add 'value'.)

Simply stated, in order **to understand how a business works** (or a sub-set of a business), we simply need to (consistently) **answer the five questions: Who does What work with Which information, and Where and When do they do it (for a given purpose – Why).**

So, for the first time perhaps in the history of commerce, we have questioned what a business/organization is fundamentally comprised of, and come up with a new, simple, almost intuitive foundational business definition.

Let's refer to these five questions as the **W5**. Now, let's test this foundation to see if it makes sense. Well, the authors run a multi-million-dollar business and, as business leaders, does it make sense for them to know *Who* is doing *What*, and *Where* and *When* they are doing the work, and *Which* information they use to do the jobs? And, are all of these *dimensions* being performed to accomplish a predefined and agreed (specific) *business purpose (Why?)*? Heck, yeah! Double heck, yeah!

In fact, it's actually kind of a stupid question! Of course, we need these questions answered, it's what we and every business leader/practitioner *has to know* to operate any business. How can you operate a business if you *don't know* the answers to these five simple questions?

In the past we have addressed these dimensions intuitively or, at best, partially (with 20th-century tools/technology).

Perhaps now we can address these questions more overtly? But does this W5 view hold up to a multi-billion-dollar Fortune 500 telecommunications company?

Absolutely. For a given purpose: 'Provide POTS (Plain Old Telephone Service)', this approach was used to explicitly define/depict all work activities (*What?*), all the human resources (*Who?*), all information (*Which?*) needed to accomplish the purpose (*Why?*), at all locations (*Where?*) where the work took place and, lastly, in all the major time frames (*When?*) that governed when the work must get done.

Essentially, massive business complexity was viewed through this five-dimensional 'prism', and within a very, very short space of time, business professionals were gaining *new insights* and *perspective* on this *very complex business* that had never been ***defined/depicted*** (end to end) in literally 100 years! Yes, they had of course seen some of these views/dimensions of the business in **isolation** but never **all five dimensions explicitly described**, and definitely never **all holistically connected!**

So think about it, there really is **nothing further needed to understand business operations**. If I know the answer to these five (deceptively) simple questions, *I will have a **comprehensive** and **complete understanding** of **how** my business operates.*

How do current business depiction tools measure up to this five-dimensional view of the enterprise?

Well, process maps/definitions clearly correlate to the business activities (*What*), and IT definitions in the past have emphasized the need for understanding information (*Which*): many consultants and organization specialists harp on about aligning work (*What*) to roles (*Who*) – the now infamous RACI (Responsible/Accountable/Consulted/Informed) charts.

But no one (up 'till now, that is), has explicitly and holistically identified all of these five business dimensions as being the foundation for any and every organization.

3.1 Purpose-based thinking

There is something missing however. Many theorists (Porter, Rockart, etc.) have for decades promoted the notion of **value added** work. That is, if work does not directly contribute value to a business (process) or *value chain* (Porter), it should not exist.

This makes tons of sense, of course. But let's expand upon this 'value added' notion. Let's agree that all five dimensions need to add value, not just the work (the 'What' in our terms). Let's also align all dimensions with a given goal or business purpose and then further agree that achieving the purpose is the *only reason* that the five business dimensions exist.

This implies that any work that does not exist to support a stated purpose is non-value added and is therefore redundant. Let's further assume the same goes for the remaining four dimensions. If the work is redundant, so potentially is the *person* doing the work, the *information* needed, the *location* and even the *time frame* governing when the work gets done.

We now have the ability to explicitly identify, in a very detailed and granular fashion, the 'things' in an organization that indeed **add** (or do not add) **value** to accomplish a given business purpose.

The *purpose* of the W5 (*What, Who, Where, When* and *Which*) is, in essence, the very reason they 'exist'. The purpose (or as we refer to it, the **purpose statement**) is the '*Why?*' It is the reason *why the work happens,* performed by *human resources* (*or machines*), at a specific *place*, using (consuming and/or producing) *information*, at a given point in *time*. Or, stated from a different perspective, **the W5s solely exist to support the attainment of the business purpose.**

This brings a new, yet very intuitive, perspective to understanding the business. It means that we now have *a succinct starting point from which to describe business operations, oblivious to organization barriers, so long as we have a* **clear purpose (or sub-purpose) statement.**

We no longer need to struggle with identifying the elusive 'start' and 'end' of a process or value chain. We simply *anchor* all work activities to the purpose statement. It either supports the purpose (fits) or doesn't. The result is binary. *Indeed, we never before could clearly isolate business processes because we had little to aid us in containing or limiting business scope.*

So far, we have introduced a brand-new way of thinking about business complexity. Different from anything before, yet viscerally familiar. We now recognize that, in order to better understand massively complex business operations, it makes (intuitive) sense to 'break down' this complexity into five 'base' or foundational dimensions (the W5). Further, we proposed the notion of **Purpose Based Thinking**™, to ensure that the five dimensions of a business domain exist for a *specific, predetermined purpose.*

The good news is that we appear to have a solid definition of the 'atomic' dimensions of any business. In other words, *a sound, intuitive framework, which will aid in the understanding of business complexity.* The bad news is that this 'framework' (i.e. breakdown of business complexity into five 'atomic' elements/dimensions) is just a starting point!

The big question is: How do we *answer* the W5 questions?

3.2 How we answer the W5 questions

It turns out that rules are indeed our *friends*!

Another *foundational flaw* with classical business/process definition or knowledge representation methods is the fact that the *diagrams created are not based on any formal 'rules' or theory.* In other words, we have attempted to describe business with text/words and crude 'boxes and arrows', with some standardized symbology, to perhaps denote decisions; and often times 'swim lanes', denoting some aspect of work responsibility and ownership at a simplistic level.

Also, let's agree that almost all the other disciplines (engineering, architecture, physics, chemistry, building science, etc.) have learned over the ages that complexity is best described with **pictures**. Words do not cut it. Words and text are informal, biased, subject to interpretation, lengthy and ambiguous, not to mention impossible to truly analyze. Simply put, *text cannot and should not be used to describe complexity* of any sort, whether it is a Boeing 777, an Intel Pentium chip or the Quote to Order business of a national telecommunications company.

The statement 'A picture is worth a thousand words',[2] has never been truer. We simply must have the capability to 'paint a picture' that captures all the pertinent information about the part or whole of the business being described. Pictures provide natural and intuitive clarity and comprehension. So, let's agree that *pictures have obvious and significant advantages in describing complexity* over text or even numbers.

Many *20th-century* business depiction/definition approaches have indeed assumed this to be the case. As a result, many approaches represented business in the form of 'boxes and arrows'. Unfortunately, besides not thinking about the foundational structure of the business and hence what they were attempting to describe, there is nothing available to *assure that what we put into the boxes has consistent meaning*. In other words, it's free-format 'art' and highly subjective.

Yes, in some few instances, the industry experts introduced 'rules' that governed the symbology of the business depiction. For example, they defined the shape of the box and attached

---

[2]'Un croquis vaut mieux qu'un long discours' (Napoleon).

some meaning to the shape (activity, decision or organization role perhaps) but *they failed to introduce rules that govern how to create content* that populates the box/symbol. This is, for the most part, intuitive and subject to the author's 'style'. You might say such approaches lack science or rigor and can be classified as nothing more than 'junk science'.

This is, of course, problematic. *What is needed is a set of rules, akin to grammar, that guide and govern the content* residing inside *of the symbols in the diagrams (picture).*

Natural language consists of a **framework** (verbs, nouns, pronouns, adjectives, adverbs, conjunctions, etc.) with a **formal set of specific rules** (called grammar) that *allows for some flexibility* in the construction of sentences, yet is still very prescriptive about the order and syntax of sentences.

Without these specific rules, language would not make any sense. Contrast a string of words without grammar, to a string of work activities described without rules! And in this comparison, we are only using *one dimension of the business* (activities), akin to *trying to use only verbs* in a sentence. Impossible! You will generate meaningless babble!

Similarly, we need *a set rules* (or grammar), that we can use to *answer the questions posed by W5 dimensions* in our businesses.

The **W5 framework** plus the associated *rules* with a formal *notation and syntax*, also allows some freedom, in terms of the construction of a **business model**, while being governed by our rules and notations (just like language).

We have called this 'language' of business expression, the **eXtended Business Modeling Language (xBML)**.

xBML (Version 4.1) consists of a set of approximately 56 rules that guide and govern the construction/creation of *business models*. Some of these rules are referenced in this book, and just like trying to learn a language by reading a grammar book, it is still very difficult to master xBML from this source alone. A certified xBML instructor should formally train students who wish to master this language. The learning curve extends to only a few days (a new concept for leadership, as in the past those selected to describe and plan business operations were *qualified simply by having a discernible pulse!*).

Yes, it takes some upfront (minimal) *investment* to learn xBML, but just think of the upside possibilities. These include *complete, repeatable, consistent and standardized business representations (models)*.

This is very significant. In other words, by adhering to the W5 view of business, learning the rules or 'grammar' to answer the questions, we can for the very first time (in the history of commerce) **create business models that are based more on 'science' than 'art' and are hence consistent and repeatable**. One can therefore train legions of business folk to do this, and potentially achieve quantum gains in perspectives, insights and understanding of the business as never before.

So, to summarize, we have created a new, 'disruptive' technology which enables the business to build 'rule'-based representations of complex business operations, using a five-dimensional view of the business.

4

What do genetic business models (xBML) look like?

L ONG BEFORE THE *PURPOSE DRIVEN LIFE* BY RICK WARREN appeared, the people at *BusinessGenetics* were inspiring and empowering corporate America with the **purpose-driven corporation**!

The starting point for every business model is always *a clearly defined and unambiguous purpose statement*. This sounds like stating the obvious, but it turns out it isn't. Sometimes the hardest thing to do on corporate modeling initiatives[1] is to agree on a *singular and succinct purpose*.

---

[1] The current record at BusinessGenetics for the longest duration to craft and agree on a purpose statement for a $1 billion business area took 1.5 days! This was for a US Forest Service project.

Purpose statements must be clear, to the point, able to be quantified (measured), doable and not cluttered with corporate PC (Politically Correct) statements. Importantly, purpose statements must also be *agreed* and *validated* by all key stakeholders. Purpose-based thinking is a rationalization technique for xBML – *What* models that allow us to view through multiple facets the nuclear material of any business.

Before we talk about purpose-based thinking, we need to understand **activities** and their importance in describing the organization. To put it plainly and simply, activities are king; they are the nucleus of any operational description. Without activities, you do not have a business operation.

We use activities as the backbone to describe all corporations in the world. We say that this company does this thing, or produces that product: *a company is nothing if it does nothing.* Conversely: *a company is what it does.*

Purpose-based thinking is also a rationalization process that allows us to follow the normal progression of business understanding, analysis and improvement. The normal progression of mapping out the corporate genes is one of:

1. Identifying sources of business information.

2. Capturing or gathering information about the business.

3. Organizing or structuring information about the business.

4. Synthesizing and analysis of information about the business.

5. Depicting (mapping) of information or the model of the business.

It is important to note that due to the lack of a formal business modeling/mapping discipline in the industry (or the world), there is little if any recognition that these phases of **business modeling** actually exist. This is important, in that most other business modeling techniques actually use a *depiction method* to support the capture of information. This is akin to using a hammer to secure a screw or a screwdriver to cut an orange! Clearly there is a mismatch between the tools used and the tasks at hand.

Purpose-based thinking provides an enhancement/augmentation of the *What* model rules (see below), by using the binary closure questions contained within those rules. We evolve the purpose of a set of activities to support the various phases of business modeling. Once again, these phases include the identification, capture, organization, analysis and depiction of business.

The normal evolution of business purposes, as we've discovered in our applied research over the past several years, moves from a (random) *activity grouping* purpose, to a *deliverable or outcome* purpose (what is produced by the collective activities, and then to what we call the '*true business*' purpose the very reason that the activities exist). For example, you could capture activities for an Accounts Payable Department as follows:

- *Purpose*: to be the Accounts Payable Department

- *this might evolve to a set of deliverables or outcomes purposes*

- *Purpose*: receive, approve and pay invoice

- *and then to a final (true) business purpose*

- *Purpose*: pay vendor.

We refer to this evolution as the *business rationalization of the purpose*. Rationalization occurs by applying and reapplying the binary closure question of the *'What'* model, that is: 'If we do activity X, and Activity Y, what have we accomplished?' (or what is the purpose of these activities?). In a similar manner, then, we also ask the question: 'In order to achieve the purpose, what activities must we perform?' This rationalization process begins to build a taxonomy of business activity or a taxonomy of business purpose.

Most of today's approaches to business modeling/mapping fail to *distinguish* between the depiction of the process and the capturing and analysis of business information for its depiction. Yet, these are very different tasks and require different structures and rules to support them.

Purpose-based thinking allows us to follow this normal progression in an organized, structured and simple way. Whether we are capturing the business information from explicit, implicit or tacit business knowledge sources, we need a (DNA-like) structure that supports the source of the business information. *Explicit* sources of business knowledge or information might include job descriptions or methods and procedure manuals; *implicit* sources of business knowledge or information might include policies and procedures and laws and regulations; and *tacit* sources of business knowledge or information might exist in the heads of business Subject Matter Experts (humans).

Purpose-based thinking also allows us to structure the business information gathering framework to fit the source of the information, and provide the flexibility to rationalize that structure toward the true business purpose. As the purposes of the business *activity sets* move through the continuum of activity grouping to true business purpose, they provide us wih a framework to analyze the business model for completeness and consistency.

In the outcome-based or deliverable purpose state, or in the true business purpose state, we achieve a much greater objectivity and stability with respect to the set of business activities that describe the business operation at hand, at either the macro (enterprise) or micro (department) level. The structure afforded by purpose-based thinking allows us to simply analyze non-value added activities that do not support the business purpose, and observe objective patterns of work. Such objective patterns of work and activities can be used to compare different organizational functions that do the same thing; or different locations that do the same thing; or even different companies that do the same thing.

Additionally, purpose-based thinking allows us to reorganize business activities to reflect the different views or facets necessary to understand today's complex organizations. For example, you can have a view of the corporation which is operational in nature and supports its mission, vision and goals and/or objectives. You can also have a view of a subset of activities performed by the corporation for the purpose of being compliant with regulations like Sarbanes-Oxley. You might also have a view that shows those activities necessary to support strategic goals. Each of these is made possible through the application of purpose-based thinking; and each of these views reuses the same genetic material or activities.

The capturing or gathering of business information needs to be fast, accurate and complete; the organization of business information needs to be consistent, stable and simple; and the analysis of business information needs to be based on a framework that is flexible, objective and discrete. Purpose-based thinking provides support for all phases of business analysis.

Again, purpose-based thinking permits us to create a taxonomy of business activities. It takes the intangible activities that organizations perform, groups them together and allows us to construct a purpose for which the activities are completed. That purpose becomes a 'key component' of the language in the business that explicitly describes a set of intangible activities in a two-word 'handle' (or phrase) that the organization can continue to use to communicate among themselves in ways never before possible.

The result of this type of grouping also gives us a framework to analyze completeness of business activities (to support a clear business purpose), and the relevance of these activities to the business purpose. In this way, it is far easier to discern what 'adds value' (supports the purpose), and what does not add value (does not support the purpose). Purpose-based thinking follows a rationalization process, then, that supports the organization analysis and communication of the business genetic material of the complex 21st-century corporation.

Now, let's look at an example (Figure 4.1) of any **standard** (if there is any such thing **workflow model** (received from a Fortune 500 company). In this example, you can see some activities arranged in a traditional (20th-century) workflow. The business activities contain whatever, that is they contain random snippets of consciousness, presumably extracted from business Subject Matter Experts by a 'process artist'. If you can't understand this model, do not fear; you will see that it makes no sense at all! It appears just as a sequence of random 'activities' connected together in time for the purpose of 'remote backflush' (whatever that is). Remember too that this is a bona fida example from a large Fortune 500 corporation!

By taking these same activities and arranging them in a purpose-based *What* model, and asking the questions stated above, we arrive at a much more comprehensible and simple representation of the business domain at hand. Even without a full comprehension of the rules associated with the *What* model (see the next section of this book, which will provide some guidance on how to read these genetic models), we

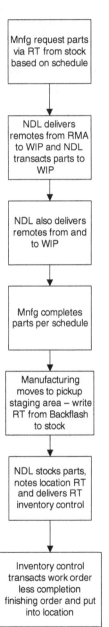

Remote backflush

Mnfg request parts via RT from stock based on schedule

NDL delivers remotes from RMA to WIP and NDL transacts parts to WIP

NDL also delivers remotes from and to WIP

Mnfg completes parts per schedule

Manufacturing moves to pickup staging area – write RT from Backflash to stock

NDL stocks parts, notes location RT and delivers RT inventory control

Inventory control transacts work order less completion finishing order and put into location

Figure 4.1   One-dimensional process flow.

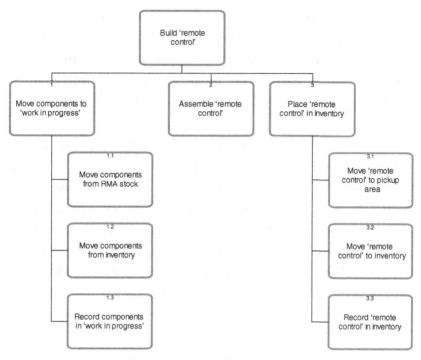

Figure 4.2   xBML *What* model.

suspect that you will find the model in Figure 4.2 far easier to understand.

During the identification and capturing of activities, and the gathering of the activities, purpose-based thinking allows us to structure information about the business in a *natural* way with respect to the source. By that, we mean that if the source is a person or business practitioner, we can capture the information based on what that person does. If the source of the information is a policy, we can capture the information for the purpose of compliance with the policy. This flexible yet stable (and reusable) genetic structure provides for a very rapid acquisition of business information.

During the organization and analysis phases of the business modeling process, purpose-based thinking enables us to see missing activities or non-value added activities in a very obvious way. A participant in an xBML-based initiative is quoted as saying: 'It makes stupid things look stupid.'

To further guide practitioners through the process of articulating purpose statements, we have developed a set of **rules**, which guide us through the creation of a **valid purpose statement**. These rules are easy to comprehend and enable business modelers to guide the business in creating meaningful and accomplishable purpose statements, the starting point of every xBML business model. Here is a table (with real examples) of before-and-after purpose statements.

Un-purposed 'process'	Purposed-based business 'process'
i. Quote-to-order	i. Sell products
ii. Provisioning	ii. Provision of telephone service
iii. Risk management	iii. Mitigate banking risk
iv. Forest planning	iv. Create forest plan
v. Outage	v. Maintain nuclear reactor

So, the business of creating an xBML business model *always* begins with a clear and agreed to purpose. For the record, purpose statements are a concrete mechanism and powerful tool to ensure alignment with corporate strategy.[2]

---

[2] xBML has successfully been used at one of the major telecommunications companies to explicitly define corporate strategy and, subsequently, to 'translate' such strategy into operational xBML business models.

So once a clear, unambiguous and succinct **purpose statement** (yes, there are more rules for creating purpose statements), has been defined and agreed to, we can begin to answer the **W5** (genetic) questions. To answer each of the questions we have created a *unique set of rules* (and techniques).[3] The result of applying these rules and techniques will be the representation of the five business dimensions (using predefined symbology) in the form of a picture or model.

To conclude, purpose-based thinking supports all phases of business process modeling. More importantly, using purpose-based thinking, we can improve the efficiency and effectiveness of all phases of the process modeling. The phases, again, are to identify and capture organization knowledge, and synthesize, analyze and then depict that knowledge. Purpose-based thinking allows us to quickly capture the complete business information, together with rapid and objective analysis and multifaceted views of the information.

Let's walk through each of the *W5* dimensions, and provide an example of the 'picture' created by applying the xBML rules.

W1: the *What* dimension

The *What* **model** serves as *the central foundation* of a business model. Simply stated, this model **depicts all** *work activities*

---

[3] These xBML rules and techniques can be learned by practitioners by attending training classes held by certified xBML training organizations.

that occur (or need to occur) to attain a given purpose statement. So, this model will determine for a given purpose – for example, 'Procure items' – all the work that must happen/ could happen to procure items.

The model uses simple 'decomposition' or 'composition' theory to break down complex tasks/work into more detailed tasks/work – breaking these tasks/work into successively more levels of details.

So a (high-level) **complex task** gets decomposed or broken down into subordinate tasks. For example, to 'Procure items', the business must:

1. Forecast item demand

2. Select vendors

3. Obtain quotation

4. Place orders

5. Receive items

6. Safeguard items

7. Account for transaction, etc.

A conceptual example of a What model is presented in Figure 4.3.

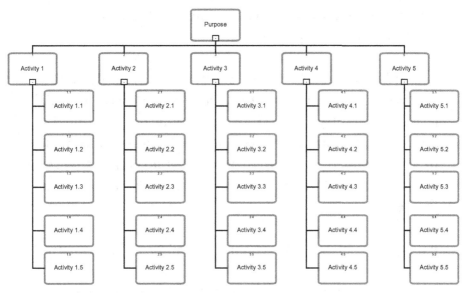

Figure 4.3 *What* model example.

Thereafter, the 'logic' associated with this model is simply *recursive*. That is, any task/work activity is viewed as a 'sub-purpose' and is further decomposed into more detailed levels of tasks/work. For example, 'Select vendor' can be broken down into the following tasks/work:

1. Identify potential vendors

2. Determine vendor criteria

3. Evaluate vendor

4. Execute vendor master service agreement, etc.

This is repeated to whatever level of detail is useful, as dictated by the project purpose.[4]

So a *What* model will yield a *complete* and very detailed (if required) *hierarchical list of all the work* (at many potential levels of detail) performed (or that could be performed) to accomplish the purpose statement. If we also state this model in mathematical terms, we have created *a complete mathematical set of all work/tasks required to accomplish a given purpose*:

$$P = T1, (T1.1, T1.2, \ldots, T1.n \ (Tn.1 \ldots Tn.n)) \ T2, T3, T4, \ldots, Tn.$$

where P = Business purpose and T = Tasks and sub-tasks. These tasks/activities are doable, quantifiable and discrete tasks/work that are *actionable* and will result in things actually getting done! There is no vagueness about this model, unlike similar, but very different, 'function' modeling (functions equate more to organizational units).

This model is practical, uncluttered and clear-cut, doable and easy to understand. It is read from top to bottom, and it is simple for anyone in the business to comprehend.

The model indeed seems so simple, but it is incredibly powerful in helping deal with massive complexity in logical (memory) 'chunks'. It also neatly and naturally *layers* **the**

---

[4] BusinessGenetics has created a very powerful and formal method for applying xBML to define/configure projects (e.g. a business improvement project, etc.). The very same method and associated rules can fruitfully be applied to support project managers in defining projects. This a large subject in its own right and one for a subsequent in-depth publication.

levels of work complexity from highest to lowest. That is, this models group levels of similar work effort together (in the same 'set'). Appendix A shows another example of a *What* model. This model is a fairly straightforward representation of how to hire a new employee (or how to fill a position).

The *What* model is truly (intuitively) simple. However, behind the scenes, there is rather more complexity. Unlike other business modeling approaches, we have invented *a set of rules* to make sure that we can teach folk in the organization to build these models in a *consistent and repeatable* manner. We (currently) have 12 rules that help you to build the *What* model.[5] Examples of some of the rules include:

Rule 1: Every *What* model activity (and every business activity therein) must explicitly support a well-defined, specific and quantifiable purpose statement.

Rule 2: Every task must be doable, hence it must consist of a Verb (first) and a Subject/Object (second).

Rule 3: Descriptive adjectives or adverbs are *not permissible* (e.g. words like 'efficient', 'optimal', 'timely', 'immediately' or 'profitably'.

Rule 4: *No other business dimensions* may be represented in this model (e.g. job roles/titles, locations, frequency).

Rule 5: *Sequence of activities* in this model is unimportant.

---

[5] The rules associated with the *What* model and all other xBML dimensions can be learned by attending a training class conducted by xBML-certified training organizations.

This *What* model will generate a complete 'mathematical' set of all the work that must, could or should occur to accomplish a *predetermined business purpose*. The model also 'layers' work into *successive layers of detail*, representing all work with a roughly *equivalent amount of effort* at the same level, thereby *avoiding 'level mixing'* issues associated with traditional process maps – e.g. 'Provision equipment' activity at the same process level as 'Cutting a check' process activity (no kidding!).

This model is the **foundational and pivotal (anchor) model**, which we will use to identify and depict all the other business dimensions (*Who, Where, Which, When*).

W2: the *Who* dimension

Now that we know *explicitly and completely* what tasks/activities the organization must do to accomplish a given *purpose statement*, it is a simple extension to identify *who is going to do the task/work*. Every single activity on the *What* model must be allocated to someone (or some role) to ensure that it gets done.

So, the *Who* model uses the *core 'building blocks'* or activities from the *What* model, and simply entails allocating an organizational unit/role/person (*Who*) in the organization that is/will be responsible/accountable for doing the *What* activity (work).

The only complexity here is that we can have *more than one* organizational unit/role/person assigned to activities in the organization. Well, that is OK, because that's (complex) reality. This model will allow us to identify *who is ultimately responsible* for actually doing the work on the *What* model, as well as those in the organization that may be *accountable* for the work. Other *Who* relationships (for example, *Who is consulted* when the task is done; *Who is informed* when the task is done; etc.) can also be depicted on this model.

Once we have identified *who* is responsible and/or accountable for all the individual tasks/work outlined in the *What* model, we need to structure or organize this model in order to better understand reporting structures.

The end-state of the model somewhat resembles an **organization chart**. However, an important difference is that this is not exactly an organization chart: it is a *sub-set* of an organization chart. It only represents those (*who*) organizational units/roles/persons (and their reporting relationship) responsible/accountable for *accomplishing the activities required to attain* the stated purpose statement of the *What* model.

In essence, it is rather a 'pure' organization chart. It focuses purely on *who* does the *work* in the *What* model: it ignores organization stovepipes, boundaries and reporting structures. It simply states, in an unbiased fashion, all the *whos that do (will do) the work in the What model.*

Examples of the *Whos* in this model may include:

1. Procurement Division

2. Procurement Manager

3. Procurement specialist

4. Vendor Manager

5. Vendor management specialist

6. Contracting Officer.

Again, we have created a half-dozen *easy-to-understand rules* that will guide business modelers through the process of consistently and completely creating a *Who* model. Examples of some of the rules associated with *Who* model creation include:

Rule 1: Each *What* must be assigned at least one corresponding organizational unit/role/person responsible and/or accountable for execution of the activity.

Rule 2: Organizational units can consist of internal or external organizations, divisions, departments, teams or job positions.

Rule 3: Reporting relationships between the *Whos* must be depicted.

We now have a comprehensive list (another 'mathematical' set) of all the parties who are responsible/accountable for *all activities*, for a given organization's purpose statement.

We are getting somewhere! For many corporate initiatives or departments, if we just had these two 'dimensions': *who does what, clearly spelled out,* we might even declare (a small) victory! And we indeed have done so for some corporations, the remaining three xBML dimensions were viewed as an added bonus!

Figure 4.4 presents an example of a simple *Who* model. Appendix A has another example of the *Who* model associated with the filling-a-position *What* model.

W3: the *Where* dimension

Work gets done at a place. That is, we have *physical* (or virtual) *places where we conduct business*. It is highly useful to identify these 'places', and clearly identify the *geographies where we do tasks/work*.

So, for each task/work activity on the *What* model we can list all the physical 'geographies' where we do/could do the work. These locations could be on a global scale (e.g. we 'Develop software' in Mumbai, India), national scale (e.g. we 'Manage IT demand' in Charlotte, North Carolina), local scale (e.g. we 'Release software' at 1801 California Street, Denver, Colorado) or at a very detailed level (e.g. we 'Pick inventory' (a *detailed What*) from Bin location 17B-4a (a *detailed Where*)). The fact is, all activities/tasks must be assigned one or more geographic locations, telling us *where the work happens or occurs*.

In our procurement example – and, again, by systematically working through the tasks/work identified in the *What* model – we can *identify all locations/places where we perform that task/work*. The locations may look like this:

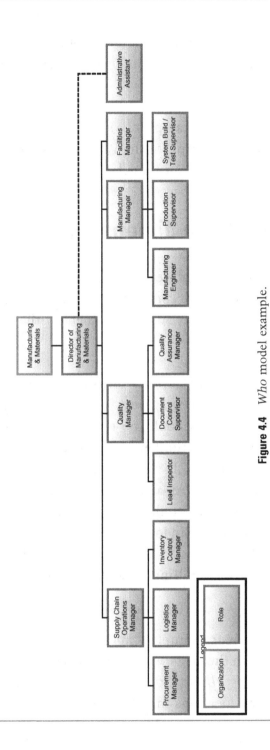

Figure 4.4 *Who* model example.

1. North America

2. Western United States

3. Kingston Court, Englewood, CO

4. Dowling Court Warehouse

5. Warehouse bin 17B-4a, etc.

Once we have identified all places or geographic locations where we do work, we can also show relationships between geographies (a simple task). That is, we can show that Dowling Court is in the Western United States and that is, of course, part of North America, etc.

This model will provide us with a *complete* ('mathematical' set) of all the geographic locations where the work (in the *What* model) is performed. We have also developed some simple **rules** (six in this case) to aid business modelers in creating a *Where* model that shows all the locations where tasks/work is/can be performed. Examples of some of the xBML rules associated with creating a *Where* model include:

Rule 1: Work (geographic) locations for each task on the *What* model must be identified.

Rule 2: Organizational units are not permissible (they are represented on the *Who* model).

Rule 3: Relationships between locations can be represented

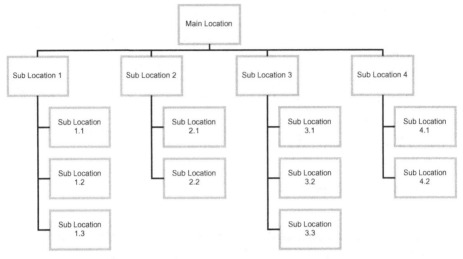

Figure 4.5 *Where* model example.

A conceptual example of a *Where* model is presented in Figure 4.5.

We have now added another important piece of information (dimension) to our complex business 'puzzle'. We have represented who does what work in the organization (to accomplish a given purpose) and we now know where all the work is done! Appendix A shows an example of a *Where* model. Later we briefly discuss what significant business decisions can be made (for example, *what* work do we do at an offshore location) by means of this model.

W4: the *Which* dimension

Past attempts to define how business operates often neglected one very critical aspect of business, namely information. *Information is the undisputed lifeblood of the 21st-century corporation.*

Our IT colleagues have long known this. A critical aspect of system design is understanding (business) information needs and relationships. IT folk have for years created vast models of data/information *requirements* and there are innumerable approaches, theories and tools to aid in this quest.

Understanding what the *business requires* to be automated (in other words, business requirements) is a whole other ball of wax. (**This challenge is the undisputed king of corporate confusion and frustration!**) This fatally flawed phenomenon will be the subject of brief discussion later in this book, but it warrants an entire publication of its own. But here is a teaser! *xBML models can be used to directly extract and **automatically** generate robust and complete business requirements.* A proven and verifiable fact! More to follow.

One fundamental flaw in past approaches is that *linking information to the business tasks is usually completely ignored!* Duh! Well, it turns out that there is indeed *a very close relationship* between tasks/work and information. *In fact, no work can happen unless information is consumed and/or produced.*

Think about it. Take any task in a business, say, 'Acquire customer' (note we use the Verb + Subject *What* model rule).

To actually do this work, you will have to know certain 'things': you will probably have to know at least the following in order to do this activity/work:

1. Prospective customers.

2. Prospect contact telephone number.

3. Existing client details.

4. Prospect type.

In fact, you cannot do the work *unless you have access to this information*. Therefore, understanding all the 'pieces' of information that will enable (or inhibit) work to be performed *is absolutely critical*.

Of course, once we know *which information* is needed to do our work, we understand which databases (and associated systems) are used/required – another extremely useful insight.

As a direct result of doing the *What* task/work at hand, you will in fact have created or changed or updated some information. In this case, you will probably have created or changed or updated the following information:

• Prospective customer

• Existing clients

• Client type.

And so another 'missing link' in understanding our business complexity is identified. We now know that *work cannot be done unless we have information available.*

To identify which information is required, we review the tasks/work in the *What* model and simply ask: which information is needed (consumed and produced, or input and output[6]) for each activity in the *What* model to be performed.

In our procurement example, we may agree that the following pieces of information must be forthcoming in order to do the tasks/work at hand:

- Vendor

- Product

- Product type

- Master Service Agreement

- Price list, etc.

By systematically working through each task in the *What* model and deriving the information required for this task to be executed, you will create *a complete mathematical set of all the information (Which model) the business requires to perform the work in the What model.*

---

[6]Information is often vaguely referred to as 'input' and 'output' in many 'art-based' business/process modeling approaches.

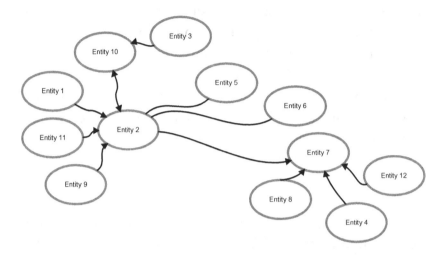

Figure 4.6 *Which* model example.

There are 14 rules to guide the business modeler through the process of creating a *Which* model (Figure 4.6). Examples of some of the rules include:

Rule 1: Information must be about *things* (e.g. Customer) or *events* (e.g. Order).

Rule 2: Pieces of information (called entities) consist of details or attributes (e.g. customer name, customer number, etc.), which describe the entity.

Rule 3: Information model must not contain data (e.g. list price versus $12.50).

Rule 4: Links or relationships between information entities can be described and documented, etc.

Appendix A has a *Which* model associated with filling a position.

The Which information model provides us with another *critical* component of our complex business puzzle. It helps us understand why very often work does not happen or the results are not as expected, because the right information is not available (or, in some instances, too much disparate information is available). *The Which information model will define for us a complete ('mathematical' set) of all the various pieces of information (entities and corresponding attributes), that enable work to be performed.*

In the past, we have viewed information as an isolated 'dimension' (often a study conducted by IT), and therefore rarely *directly linked* to actual business activities at a discrete level, and in fact a better understanding of information needs was of little value to the business and even confusing.

But, of course, it makes tons of sense to conclude that *a business will not function without access to information*. We know this, but have never been able to (rapidly) understand our information needs and how they relate to work. Until now, that is!

Trust us, IT folks will usually get pretty excited if you build an xBML model and depict business activities (*What*) together with the associated 'pieces' of information (*Which*) the business requires (consumes or produces).

Our 'picture' of our complex 21st-century business is almost complete. For a given purpose (*Why*), we have now defined *Who* does *What* work, *Where* they do this work and *Which* information they require (to consume or produce). Yet another major piece of the puzzle is in place and, for the first time, slotted neatly into the business world.

W5: the *When* model

The very last thing we need to describe, to complete our understanding of our complex 21st-century business, is the chronology of work.

21CC demands an intricate choreography of work. *Timing of when work happens is often absolutely crucial.* Delay a business activity (for example, 'Approve affiliate billing journal entries' by just 2 days) and the entire 'close (financial) books' process goes to heck. Timing is everything. Perform work too soon, and the result can be equally problematic.

We have seen *sequence dependencies* of work in our now anachronistic 20th-century 'process maps'. This proves useful, but there is scant evidence of methods to help depict, understand and denote that the execution of certain work is specifically *governed by time.* That is, how do we know that a given (*What*) activity/task *must occur at exactly this point in time* (e.g. in the financial close process, maybe exactly three business days before we close the books)? It is absolutely essential that we start to get an understanding of the time frames that govern and dictate *when* work must occur.

We find that *business operates in accordance with all kinds of calendars or time frames.* These time frames govern or dictate our work far more often than we realize.

What do we mean by 'time frames'? Some examples of time frames that 'govern' our business may serve to illustrate:

- *Calendar time*: the good old Gregorian calendar (with all of its associated time units: decades, years, quarters, months, weeks, days, hours, seconds, etc.).

- *Fiscal time*: financial calendars (financial year, financial quarter, financial periods, etc.).

- *Production shifts time*: manufacturing or production time frames (shifts, manufacturing cycles, etc.).

- *Service-level time*: product-support time frames.

- *Business-cycle time*: Planning time frames.

- *Regulatory time*: Sarbanes-Oxley legislation, for example, dictates annual financial control reporting time frames.

Timing is everything. Yet we have lacked a method for even recognizing the many time frames that govern and control our business!

We have 'invented' a new way of identifying and describing the time frames that govern our organizations. There are six **rules** to guide the business modeler through the process of creating a *When* model.

Examples of some of the *When* model rules include:

Rule 1: All time frames must be able to be reconciled against calendar time.

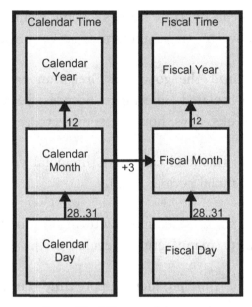

Figure 4.7 *When* model example.

Rule 2: Time frames must consist of one or more time units/periods.

Rule 3: Time units/periods are composable/decomposable.

A time model is depicted in Figure 4.7.

This model helps us to identify, describe and better understand *all the pertinent time frames* (and detailed time units/periods) *that govern the execution of work* in our corporations (but not necessarily *work sequence*). We will show you in the next section how we depict the connection between *temporal governance* and *sequential work execution*. There is another example of a time or *When* model in Appendix A.

Understanding *when* work must or should occur can bring powerful insights and understanding regarding (re)sequencing tasks, or enforcing that certain tasks occur at the correct time, so as not to delay downstream work.

So, now we have a complete five-dimensional view of our business. We have isolated each of the **W5s** and grouped our complex business into these five logical categories. After this 'dissection' of our complex business, we can begin to understand *how* these five dimensions are interrelated.

W5I (Integrated): the *How* model

By Jove, we've done it! We have a means to represent our business complexity in its entirety. We have systematically broken down potentially massive business complexity into five (and only five) simple business dimensions (categories):

1. Activities (*What*)

2. Responsibilities (*Who*)

3. Localities (*Where*)

4. Information (*Which*)

5. Timing (*When*).

We have a *complete and meaningful* (atomic or genetic) understanding of the organization in its entirety! Foundationally, there is nothing else to describe.

The corporate 'gene' is exposed! We are now able to understand and even 'genetically engineer' our business, with these
strands of corporate DNA. Aspects like 'How much?' merely
measure resource consumption of one or more of these business 'dimensions'; systems merely automate one or more of
these dimensions. And capital enables them. So, armed with
this business description/definition, we can see, in terms we
can all relate to, *how the business truly operates*. To completely describe or depict a business, there is little else (perhaps
nothing) that we need to know!

By recognizing that a business consists of these five dimensions, we are able to *break down inherent complexity*. By
applying the 56 or so xBML rules, we are able *to answer these
simple questions consistently*. And the result of answering
the questions in accordance with the rules consistently *produces a diagrammatic representation* of our business that
anyone (with minimal training) can intuitively understand
or 'get'.

Well, this 'systematic' representation of our business already
has many, many obvious uses, for example:

- business improvement

- job definitions

- system-to-business connectivity

- business requirements definition

- foundation for costing

- understanding regulatory compliance

- efficiency analysis.

But more on this later.

What we are not able to see in our five-dimensional view of the business is the *interaction or interconnectivity between these five dimensions*. Just like other disciplines, say, biology or physics, we have 'broken down' immense complexity into small (atomic) self-contained units (like atoms or DNA components). And just like biologists or physicists, now that we have *extraordinarily detailed insights and understanding of the essence of the business, we can reconstitute and sequence these elements into a representation of how these 'pieces' fit together*, thus depicting how the business operates at many levels. This is exactly how physicists and biologists understand massively complex 'systems', and exactly how we can better understand business complexity.

First, *dissect the complexity into simplistic 'atoms'*, or the **W5s**. Once we completely understand (almost intuitively) these more simply represented dimensions of the business, we are able to *see how they fit together and operate as a whole*.

We, in fact, diagrammatically 'snap' the pieces we have described together, into what we call a *How* model (see Figures 4.8–4.10). The W5 'atomic' dimensions are *simply connected, sequenced and assembled* to 'configure' a *How* model.

As you can see, the *How* model is centered around the *What* model (or work activities). This is important because the way

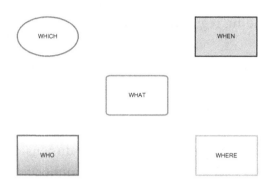

Figure 4.8 *How* model components.

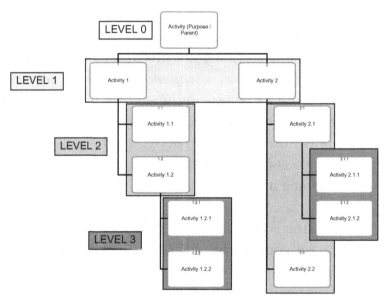

Figure 4.9 Selecting *How* model level of detail.

we created the *What* model was by means of (de)composition theory. That is, we broke down high-level purpose statements into a structured, grouped *layer of tasks* required to perform the purpose. We then continued to *recursively break down work into successive groups (mathematical sets) or layers of work (detailed sub-sets)*. Consequently, we have conveniently

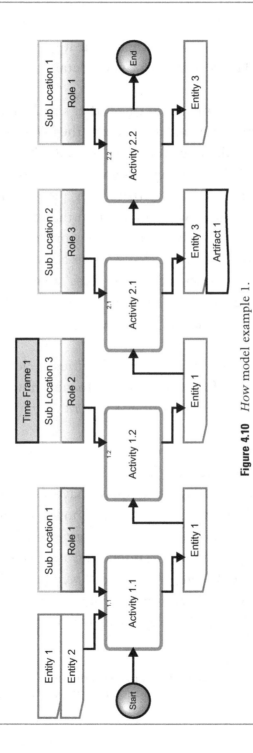

Figure 4.10 *How* model example 1.

grouped all work (from a high to a low detail level) into 'equivalent' layers or levels of work detail.

Another way to think about this is that *similar levels of work effort* are represented at each layer in the *What* model. These levels of 'equivalent' work can conceptually be represented as in Figure 4.11. This is very useful as one of the significant issues encountered with 20th-century process 'art' was the fact that work levels were, more often than not, mixed (level mixing). We often mixed high-level work or activities (e.g. 'Plan inventory') with detailed work or activities (e.g. 'Count stock'). Clearly, 20th-century 'process' maps had no technique to guide the author through a 'leveling' exercise. The results were often unusable.

Since we have leveled our work activities in 'levels of detail' of approximate effort, we can decide to view *how the business operates at each and any or every work level* (Figure 4.11).

In fact, it is a relatively simple and almost mechanical process to represent 'workflows', with all five business dimensions *(at any level, 1 through n[7])*. All we have to do is *select the relevant level of detail* from a *What* model, which should be dictated, in the first place, by *the purpose of building the business model* and then simply and almost mechanically attach the *Who*, *Where*, *Which* and *When* dimensions to each *What*, or activity. Thereafter, it's a simple process of *sequencing the activities (Whats)* and *depicting workflow*.

---

[7] Sorry, but there is no good reason to arbitrarily limit the number of work levels to three or four as some of the 'flat-earthers' in the process world have us believe.

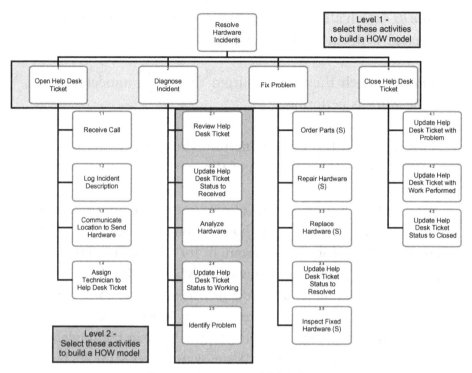

Figure 4.11 *How* model leveling.

Once we have ascertained the relevant level of detail for our *How* model, we, again, have a set of simple ***rules*** to guide us through the process of creating one:

Rule 1: Represent/select all work activities for a given level in the *What* model.

Rule 2: Sequence each activity in terms of predecessor and successor tasks (note that some tasks may occur simultaneously or have no predecessors or successors).

Rule 3: Attach all information (from the *Which* model) that is created/updated as a result of doing the work.

Rule 4: Attach all responsibilities (from the *Who* model) associated with the activity (from the *What* model).

Rule 5: Attach the location (from the *Where* model) where the work is performed.

Rule 6: Attach the time frame/unit (from the *When* model) that governs the execution of the work.

The result is a more stable (almost mechanically produced) and leveled model depicting *how* the business operates, with all five 'dimensions' represented for the given business purpose. The *How* model shows us *who* is doing *what* with *which* information, and *when* and *where*, in one comprehensive business view. This representation is easily constructed, especially if 21st-century technology is used in the modeling process (for example, the xBML Innovations (xBMLi) W5 business model editor).

Just as geneticists need to keep track of extremely complex DNA strands, so we as business modelers need **advanced (software) tools** to help track this complexity. Advanced technology, like the xBMLi W5 business model editor, is a very necessary component of capturing business complexity in a database of the business. This enables us to actually store and use this business knowledge in the powerful and accessible *XML* database!

Figure 4.12 presents another simple example of a *How* model (and see Appendix A for an example associated with the 'Fill position' model). This *How* model (for a given level, say, level

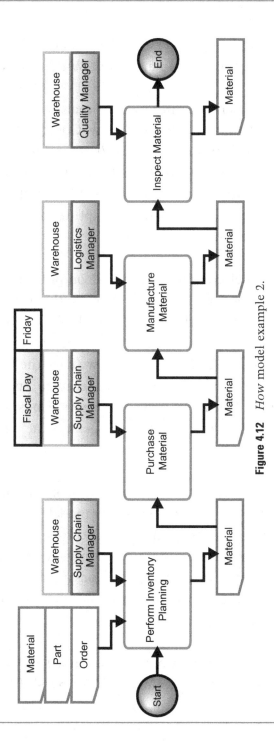

Figure 4.12 *How model example 2.*

2 of the *What* model) depicts *What* work is performed by *Who*, and *Where* and *When* and with *Which* information.

Of course, matters are more easily managed if knowledge *linkages* (for example, the Beer Flow Coordinator (*Who*) is responsible for distributing) beer (*What*) and needs to know, 'Beer type and order' (*Which*)) between the dimensions are *electronically stored* (and 'remembered' for ever) by the business model editor, as you record/capture this information about the business.

The *How* model comprises the final *output*, of completely describing the business. In order to create this important representation of the business, we first broke down business complexity into its basic 'dimensions', akin to gathering and sorting all of our Lego® blocks. Once we have the information gathered, structured and sorted, it's easy to snap together long (business DNA) 'strands' representing business operations (showing how the business operates, at any level of complexity).

We avoided the trap of attempting to depict business complexity by trying to create first a *How* model. We consciously stepped back and identified the *W5* components and then assembled a far more accurate and complete *How* model (or process representation). This approach assures far more meaningful, complete and accurate business depictions at *multiple levels* of detail.

The business representations are all based on a common, simple and yet intuitive framework (the 5Ws). Furthermore, we have applied a set of formal rules, which help us to deliver a representation of the business that is complete, consistent and (relatively) easy for the business to understand.

Lastly, we are able to snap together more accurate representations of how our business operates in the form of a *How* model. This model is 'automatically' leveled, purpose based and able to depict all five dimensions of the business.

We now have the stuff to start depicting the very genes of the corporation and, of course, the ability to proactively define our business future!

5

How do we (quickly) create xBML models (aka Business Co-Formulation™)

PLEASE PAY ATTENTION HERE, FOR THE CONCEPT WE introduce below can potentially save gargantuan amounts (yes, we mean it) of resource (translating into many millions of dollars, really!).

To illustrate the point, here is a true 'war' story. Freshly arrived from across the pond, and as eager as a beaver, one of the authors convinced a VP of a large RBOC (Regional Bell Operating Company) to model the finance organization using xBML (or more accurately, a crude and simplistic first version thereof).

Following is the 'war' story as related by one of the authors.

The VP agreed that this **multi-dimensional, rule-based business definition/depiction methodology** was by far superior to the crude Visio® charts and simplistic Rummler-Brache 'swim-lanes' that a 'final four' (green bean) consultancy had previously created (for a small fortune, of course), and hence we ventured forth . . .

The first interactive work session, with around 18 seasoned finance SMEs (Subject Matter Experts) was, to say the least, very, very memorable. I began by explaining the **W5** business dimensions and some of the base **xBML** rules, seeded with a few simple examples of xBML models. So far, so good. This 'orientation' and SME education took about 30 minutes and the participants seemed skeptical but intrigued, and at least mildly engaged. So they indulged me for a while . . .

That's when all holy hell broke loose! I made (in hindsight) the fatal error of walking to the array of white boards and attempting to 'model' the finance business area with a blank canvas approach.

As soon as the SMEs perceived that I was about to do this, the work session rapidly degenerated into, literally, anarchy (plenty of eye rolling, arm crossing, disengagement, answering of pagers, etc.). I had a bona fide mutiny on my hands! I tried personality, charisma, pleading, the big management stick but frankly, my dears, they didn't give a damn.

So, how do we avoid this painful scenario at all costs?

In the past we have drawn on the most prolific but expensive source of knowledge to understand business, namely business folk or SMEs. Yes, they certainly know the business, since that's how they occupy their time every day of their professional lives, *but here's a summary of why this is a horrible idea*:

1. **SMEs in 21CC simply do not have the time** to curtail business operations and spend significant amounts of time being 'interviewed', or in laborious, time-consuming and very costly white board centered business modeling 'work sessions'.

2. **21CC is far too complex** to attempt to recall the entire minutia of details the business SMEs' job entails; there is simply too much knowledge to even remotely recall all of this knowledge.

3. **SMEs have zero tolerance** for expending large chunks of precious time trying to recall massive business complexity in the minutest detail (which they have most probably already spent at least once on previous projects or initiatives).[1]

SMEs have been there before, experience little to no return and, frankly, do not have the time, patience or tolerance in 21CC to do this yet again.

The huge lesson learned was this: the high demands of 21st-century commerce have created a situation where business SMEs have zero tolerance for almost any attempt to (re)define/depict business from scratch.

---

[1] This zero-tolerance attitude by SMEs is certainly, in part, due to historic consulting inefficiency of traditional consultancies who are, of course, largely motivated by financial performance – i.e. an hour of interview time equates to an hour of consulting revenue, so let's interview *ad infinitum*, why don't we?

Do not, we repeat *do not, attempt to create xBML models (or any other model for that matter) from a proverbial 'blank canvas' (or whiteboard).* And, of course, especially do not attempt to describe the business from a 'blank canvas' (or whiteboard) with a business methodology illiterate 'artist' disguised as a consultant/process expert in a snappy suit (or khakis to make them appear more 'folksy' – yeah, right!).

And we suppose there are many more reasons for SME *intolerance to model the business* from scratch. There are indeed multitudes of factors at play. For a further example, the business is sick and tired of folk (usually unsuccessfully) attempting to, yet again, define/depict the business. At one particular RBOC we came across 71 prior attempts to describe/depict their core POTS (Plain Old Telephone Service) business (and/ or parts thereof), and 71 sets of disposable models and output. ROM costs for the production of this output were estimated by one manager at about 1 million dollars a pop! – roughly *$70 million of disposable work!* Ouch!

The wastage here is staggering in its magnitude, especially if we extrapolate this across the rest of the enterprise, across the industry and then across the economy! Just think about that for a minute or two – and unfortunately, it gets even worse, as you will see when we discuss the 'single-use syndrome' of most business modeling output.

So the central point is that 20th-century process mapping approaches, *laboriously describing the business by way of interviews (heaven forbid) or multitudes of workshops, are simply too time-consuming.* If one plays around with some hypothetical numbers, it becomes very apparent that it is almost an impossibility to describe any sizable and complex business in a reasonable time-frame. Refer to Box 5.1 to better understand what an immense challenge it is to use 20th-century approaches for gathering business knowledge.

Box 5.1   Information Overload

Assume a business domain with only 200 human resources. Then assume that the average length of service in the business is 7 years. Now calculate the *sum of total knowledge* in that business domain (200 × 7 = 1400 years). That is, there is a total *body of knowledge of 1400 years*!

Let's (rightly) argue that a bunch of the *knowledge is repetitive* or duplicated, that is assume there are 15 folk that do AR and they all do pretty much the same thing. Let's (ridiculously) assume that we are still overestimating unique business knowledge, so we reduce our total knowledge estimate by *90%*! OK, let's say our business has even more overlap/similar work than that, and (overly) reduce the remaining 10% by *half* – that still leaves *70 years of 'unique' business knowledge.*

Regardless of this hypothetical calculation, it makes sense that a new person coming into the organization requires months (if not a year or more) to truly understand the complexity of the business.

Ergo, *it's simply way too expensive and unproductive to attempt to harvest business knowledge solely from the heads of SMEs.* Most often, it doesn't warrant the enormous cost associated with the business knowledge gathering effort, especially considering the opportunity cost of these resources who could be doing their 'real' jobs.

On the *recall front* (point 2 in the above list), think about it from a psychological perspective. If you were asked to recall on a blank sheet of paper all the details of something you do almost every day, say, driving your car from home to work, you would really struggle! It would take a lot of effort, you would *absolutely not* be able to recall all the details. You might omit many, many details such as: obeying the speed limit, or checking your gas, or checking the traffic report or checking your gas gauge, or literally a thousand other things that may be critical to a safe journey. We are sure you will see the parallel with complex business.

However, psychologically, if you were asked to *review* a picture which contained most of the details (i.e. 70%–80%) of your trip from home to work, and simply asked to fill in the missing gaps, the results and effort would undoubtedly be far more detailed and complete. And importantly, much more productive.

This is the power of review versus recall psychology. Not only more *productive* but more *SME/business-friendly*, to be sure. And if this information were presented to you in a *complete, consistent and intuitive manner* (say, xBML pictures), even better!

In 21CC no one, we repeat no one (especially over-priced consultants), should be (re)defining/depicting our business from scratch! It's simply not worth it and the business will no longer tolerate this extravagant indulgence. And there are more sound reasons that solidly support this accelerated approach for harvesting or *recycling business knowledge,* many more, but we are sure you get the point.

So, even if we have a fabulously new way of defining/depicting the business, we simply cannot tie up valuable and very costly business resources in attempting to describe business operations (from scratch). The question is where on earth do we tap into business knowledge so as not to burden the business?

Well, here's how! Information and knowledge abound. It's absolutely everywhere! You will be amazed at the (over)abundance of business knowledge sources that exist within organizations. We have found pertinent and relevant knowledge in the most unlikely of places. Of course, they are also in the obvious places like the old process maps, business plans and procedure manuals. But knowledge can also be found in PowerPoint® presentations, system documentation, job description and even application code itself. All of these sources and many more (see Appendix B for a comprehensive list of potential knowledge sources/stores) will often yield gobs and gobs of business knowledge.

Now, some will claim that there is nothing new here. They will argue that, of course, we look at existing 'documentation' at the start of the project. To be blunt, some claim to reuse existing stuff – but their claims are largely bullshit (excuse us!).[2] Existing knowledge is simply not effectively *recycled* with 20th-century approaches and is, for the most part, largely ignored.

So, why have we not recycled this knowledge before? A small minority of experienced consultants – process 'mappers', and the like – in some instances will intuitively ask for existing documentation, which they often absorb primarily as an input or aid to understanding the massive complexity of business. Their major dilemma is the lack of a *formal foundation* to make sense of this 'trapped' knowledge.

The issue is that all of these forms of knowledge are in fact tacit. That is, they are in a non-explicit format and the 20th-century business or process depiction software has created yet another source of tacit confusion (albeit, in some cases, 'artistically' accurate). The world has simply lacked a solid foundation for understanding the type(s) of knowledge that comprise a business, a *taxonomy to recycle and make sense of the chaos.*

As we have discussed, knowledge about the business genuinely abounds, it's all over the place! In fact, almost certainly, it's trapped in every desk, cupboard or credenza; it's in the storeroom and the Visio® charts (puke!), in job descriptions and user manuals and even embedded in software code. We

---

[2] If you are ever challenged on this point, simply ask the individual concerned why they still need weeks and weeks of SME facing work sessions, if they have allegedly leveraged all these knowledge sources. Trust us, that will shut them up in a heartbeat!

call this 'Scarlet Pimpernel knowledge'. It's here it's there, it's everywhere! Ha-ha!

And best of all, it's relatively 'free', or certainly very, very inexpensive to tap into (unlike the SMEs). It's also available 24×7, doesn't have an attitude, doesn't need 'bribe' dough-nuts and isn't fearful about your intent!

So, the great news is, for those that paid attention, now we have a *rule-based and consistent method of recycling unstructured business knowledge* from existing unstructured (tacit) knowledge sources. Effectively, recycling business knowledge that is free, abounds and readily available, we are able to simply 'co-formulate' this unstructured mess into the W5 format (by applying the rules), and without bothering a single business person! This is illustrated in Figure 5.1.

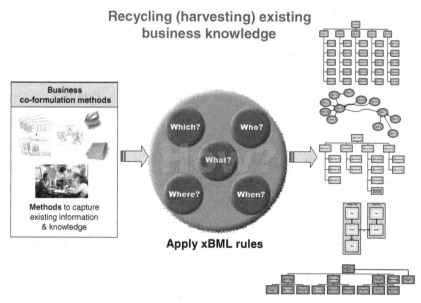

Figure 5.1 Business knowledge reuse.

Wow! Please pause here to estimate the potential productivity gain across your enterprise, by leveraging this knowledge-recycling concept (Box 5.2). We call this notion of recycling disparate and tacit knowledge sources (found in many 'business artifacts') into a structured, explicit xBML format **Document Co-Formulation**™ (DCF™). Now, let's take DCF a step further. Once we have exhausted all usable[3] tacit knowledge sources and converted this unstructured mass of knowledge into xBML format, how do we fill in the missing blanks and correct the inevitable errors?

From experience, we know that on average DCF efforts yield between 70% and 80% of the required knowledge. But how do we complete the missing 20%–30%? Or, if this is the average, what if we only generate some smaller percentage of knowledge?

Well, we have developed a notion, which we have labeled **Facilitated Co-Formulation**™(FCF™). FCF is simply an expansion of the DCF notion to embrace the business, fill in the blanks, correct the errors and 'sanction' the xBML output. Together we will call these methods Business Co-Formulation™ (BCF™)

The BCF process entails performing DCF, firstly, and then reviewing, refining and validating the xBML model with a Super-SME, someone, or some few persons who have *deep knowledge of the business domain* at hand. Once the xBML model has been *reviewed* versus recalled and validated by a

---

[3] Naturally, a sub-set of the documentation or 'artifacts' collected will not yield new or usable knowledge. Duplication may abound and some documentation may genuinely be dated.

Box 5.2   The 'Wanna be' business model

Our 'Final four' friends have made a fine living convincing us to understand our so-called *'Current-State'* or *'as-is'* *business*. The theory is, once we understand our current *'as-is'* business state, we can define a *desired state or 'to-be'* business model and then implement this new improved way of doing business.

Well, unfortunately, it sounds great but it's also BS! Firstly, *there is no such thing in corporate America as a 'current-state' or 'as-is' state.* Business is so complex or broken (or both) that *there are dozens of ways (or more) of doing business even in a single department,* all of which are inconsistent. Often, the only reason business functions is because of the departmental heroes or Super-SMEs. To attempt to understand exactly how business operates to the *n*th degree, and all the permutations of what transpires, is usually a gigantic waste of resource and energy.

We know that some very handsome consulting fees have been generated in this fashion but the return is oftentimes just not there.

But we do need to get on the same page, and soon. So, let's talk about an *'interim consensus state'* (ICS) business model. In essence, by defining the **ICS** business model, we are all getting on the same page and *agreeing that going forward this is how we will operate the business.*

No grandiose hammering away at foundationally re-engineering the corporation, just defining how we are going to operate and get *everyone* (including leadership) on the same page.

The reality is, in many instances (and, of course, there are a few exceptions here of corporations that do indeed have a firm, agreed and well-defined operating model), *this relatively small step can often yield enormous efficiencies.* For instance:

- improved understanding of the business domain by all participants

- clear delineation, definition and agreement on responsibilities

- improved cycle time/throughput (just by understanding the impact your work has on colleagues downstream).

Of course, many so-called 'future-state' business improvements efforts are, in reality, doing exactly this. And in probably 99% of cases *the simple act of defining and agreeing how we are going to work will yield numerous 'Quickwins'.* No fancy colored belts required, just focused and motivated business professionals armed with a clear and precise business definition capability.

Super-SME, *only then do business representatives engage.* Their task is simply to again review and refine the xBML model, rather than *recalling* everything they know about the business on a blank canvas. By this stage, we should have accurately modeled at least 70–80% of the business area.

The psychology of FCF is a thing of beauty! As opposed to the 'zero tolerance' effect (mentioned above), the first-time SMEs (having appreciated the fact that we are considerate of their time and maximized all other knowledge sources and business artifacts before engaging with them) *can truly engage and use their time productively,* reviewing and refining the business model. In fact some may even be fearful (for obvious reasons!) that critical aspects of the model are missing or incorrect. Human nature wants to fix the relatively small percentage (usually not more than 20%) of the xBML model that needs refinement.

So, the process of BCF consists, firstly, of leveraging existing knowledge stored in various documents or artifacts (*DCF*), and secondly, reviewing and refining the converted xBML models with a Super-SME and then a broader SME audience. This can in fact be represented in an xBML *What model* (Figure 5.2).

Of course, in certain rare instances (which in our experience are truly few and far between), it may be possible that absolutely no existing knowledge sources exist. In this instance, one should resort to either acquiring existing models (preferably already in xBML format, or industry prints); reviewing and customizing them for your environment (with Super-SMEs); and thereafter engaging with a broader SME audience.

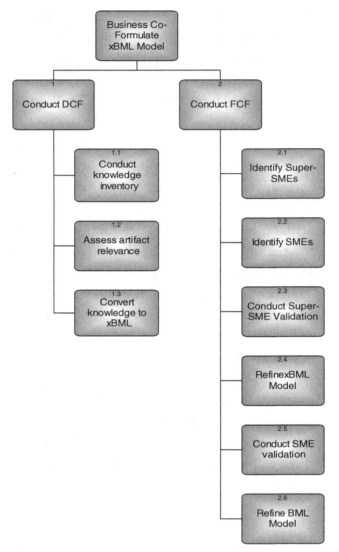

Figure 5.2 The business co-formulation *What* model.

Failing the existence of any form of business knowledge (we can't imagine how), then yes, you may have to resort to a Facilitated Co-Formulation or workshop mode to create your business model.

So this BCF notion is not only highly productive (by leveraging existing tacit knowledge), but is very useful in getting the business to truly engage, using review psychology and, most importantly, minimizing business impact.

6

The 'So what?' (where's my darn ROI?)

HERE'S ANOTHER HORRENDOUS WAR STORY. MANY years ago, while working with a global diamond company (gosh, it's hard to disguise a monopoly!), myself and a team of SMEs built an xBML (version $1^1/_2$ at the time!) mining procurement model. It was beautiful! Multidimensional and all. It brought tears to my ears and even choked up the brilliant Project Manger. He emotionally exclaimed, 'We have never done anything like this in the entire history of De Company!'

We proudly and enthusiastically presented our business models in all their five-dimensional glory to the executive sponsor team. The first 30 minutes could best be described politely as 'indulgent'. The remaining 20 minutes were unfortunately career altering.

It all started when one grizzled veteran asked me one simple question (three times actually): 'What have you done for our company?' Dry-mouthed and perspiring like Naccio at a federal hearing, I vainly attempted to answer, to no avail. The gray-haired fox told me exactly what I had done over the past seven months (pre the notion of BCF). Roughly translated but in no uncertain terms, I was told that I had squandered the equivalent of at least one person-year of business SME time, charged them in the neighborhood of $100 000 and produced a bunch of pictures (albeit much better-looking ones than he had seen from the Arthur Andersen Automatons). Pandemonium ensued; I could see the career-limiting panic in the poor PM's eyes.

A very valuable lesson was learned that day. Not only is it vital to possess a consistent, repeatable and rule-based method for defining business, but it is equally important to *do something with the models*! ROI reigns supreme in 21CC.

The good news is that there is an astounding amount that can be accomplished with xBML models. They are, however, a proverbial means to an end, and must be viewed as such.

And it's pretty remarkable stuff. A case in point is with a major nuclear power generation plant. xBML was directed toward improving the cycle time of a nuclear refueling outage, a costly and complex choreography.[1] Previous outages had

---

[1] During a refueling outage, not only does the plant lose approximately $1 million a day in lost revenue but power may have to be purchased to satisfy demand, and there is the additional cost of contract maintenance workers, also in the region of up to $1 million per day. Consequently, mandatory reactor maintenance (approximately every 18–24 months) can affect the company by as much as up to $3 million/day.

taken up to 47 days, contrasted to industry best outages (with similar reactor types) of around 20 days.

Using xBML, they were able to approach the business of a nuclear refueling outage far more 'scientifically'. The net result was a reduction in outage cycle time by as much as 25 days! With a potential enormous financial upside – well in the ballpark of a $1 million/day improvement potential.

And this is one of countless real examples of organizations that have yielded positive ROI from a relatively modest investment.

The topic of ROI appears to be somewhat of a black art. There are many, many thoughts and views. We can't possibly do this important topic full justice here and won't even attempt it; however, we will set the stage and summarize the main 'things' that clients do with xBML models to simplify/clarify/improve/ensure compliance, etc. in their respective businesses.

First, some ROI stage setting. The chart in Figure 6.1, reflects one of the frustrations associated with many Business Improvement (BI)/BPM efforts. Leadership require BI/BPM projects to deliver ROI (let's just call this Business Gain(s)), in the 'Desired return' range. That is, these projects need to deliver tons of 'Gains' (cost savings, revenue improvement, client satisfaction improvement, reduced churn, whatever) with minimal 'Pain' (costs, disruption, transformation,

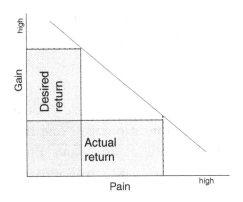

Management BI desire curve

Figure 6.1 Desired and actual return on investment.

re-skilling, re-tooling, capital investment, IT systems impact, legal, whatever).[2]

Largely because of the 20th-century tools and technology used and low skills of the BI/BPM 'specialists' (also, to a large extent, the often unrealistic expectations/desires of leadership), the actual performance is quite often in the 'Actual return' range.

No wonder BPM, BI, TQM, Six Sigma, BPR, etc. often gets a bad rap! And no wonder these tools and technologies always fall into Geoffrey Moore's 'Chasm', only to resurface a few years later with a brand-new label! But like it or not, leadership have the final say. When all is said and done, they cut the checks. So more realistically, we should think about BI/ BPM efforts along the lines of the chart in Figure 6.2. In this scenario, 'Pain' is a function of 'Gain'. Assuming we under-

---

[2] There is no space for a lengthy dissertation, so we have hugely (over)simplified ROI into Pain and Gain! But you get the picture.

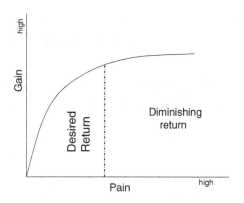

Management BI desire curve

Figure 6.2 Optimized return on investment.

stand the corporation well enough (using xBML), we should be able to yield an increasing 'Gain' almost exponentially: *the more that is 'invested' (although at a diminishing rate), the greater the 'Gain'.*

Of course, there is a (high) threshold, at some point where 'Gains' will start to diminish. So the takeaways here are fourfold:

1. *Modest gains* must be expected for *modest investment.*

2. *Increasing gains* will result with *increasing investment,* if the right tools, initial investment, infrastructure and technologies are in place and are able to be *relentlessly re-leveraged.*[3]

---

[3] There is a definitive minimum investment (Pain) that leadership must be willing to make in order to realize increasing Gain.

3. Gains and Pains must be *consciously managed, measured and monitored*, to ensure an optimized investment.

4. Recognize the *optimal threshold* of investment (by monitoring your leading metrics) and scale back when appropriate.

Pretty intuitive stuff, really – basic 101 ROI thinking, which somehow either is no longer being taught at our business schools or leadership have forgotten this basic notion (based on our experience with many Fortune 500 corporate managers).

But the challenge is, of course, how can organizations use xBML models to yield *quantifiable* and *incremental gain* (ROI), and demonstrate such gains rapidly? How do we assure incremental gains from our investment? What is the minimum investment threshold of investment in these methods, tools and technologies? All good questions, so let's get to it!

6.1 Some quantifiable types of business gain

Let's first focus on the place where most corporations start; it's usually in one or more of the areas listed below. Later, we deal with how to continue to leverage xBML models to yield continued incremental gains, as discussed above. Also, in this book we will not empower the reader to become an expert in any of the methods and techniques discussed; in fact, we will not even discuss each of the dozen or more approaches (methods and techniques) that can yield these gains. We simply summarize the most commonly deployed approaches that historically have yielded the most Gain.[4]

There are three main categories of Gains where you can leverage xBML models. Of course, there are others but these are the areas where leadership tends to relentlessly focus. The winners are:

1. Cost reduction

2. Revenue improvement

3. Increased throughput.

As much as it pains the authors, ubiquitous cost reduction is still undoubtedly the number one focus of many Fortune organizations and government bodies in the USA. This seriously flawed thinking, associated with a strategy of relentless cost cutting, is absolutely and entirely, non-sustainable. Clearly, surgical planned expense control is the preferred approach.

Based on the 30 or so Fortune companies and many government bodies that have adopted and successfully deployed xBML, we have summarized the principal methods and techniques

---

[4] Should you wish to understand all the available methods and techniques for improving ROI, and become skilled in these, again we refer you to a certified xBML training organization.

used to identify significant and so-called 'green dollar'[5] cost reductions, revenue improvement and throughput improvement, together with a brief description. (As mentioned, this is by no means a complete list of the methods and type of Gains that can be realized from an xBML model.)

With a clear and detailed **W5** understanding of the business complexity at hand, a number of additional *formal analysis methods and techniques* can be applied to the xBML models. But the methods/techniques above will usually identify much more business improvement than your organization is ready to assimilate! Additional ways of leveraging xBML models to identify Gain, include:

(a) Sourcing analysis

(b) (Five-dimensional) business cost analysis

(c) Six Sigma revitalization

(d) Service-level agreement co-formulation.

We now briefly discuss each of these.

(a) Sourcing analysis

xBML can provide a very clear understanding of a business domain which aids (out/in)sourcing decisions. Yet again, industry practices applied to make such decisions, as well as

---

[5] Improvements that have a net positive effect on the Income Statement.

Table 6.1 Summarized (principal) methods and techniques for identifying business gain

Analysis method/ type	Description	xBML dimensions used	Gain type
1. Cycle Time Analysis	Cycle times can be analyzed in terms of: (i) eliminating, reducing or automating manual work/*effort*; (ii) reducing/eliminating *work recursion*; and (iii) reducing *lag time* between work activities	All W5s but primarily the *How* model	Eliminating, reducing and automating work, together with reducing (eliminating) work recursion, usually yield *significant cost reductions* or can equate to *improved throughput* *Improved revenue* can also be realized by this analysis, because often the improved throughput will translate into processing more orders, service requests, etc. in the same (or less) amount of time
2. Affinity analyses	The method of (electronically) identifying 'intersection' points between one or more of any of the W5 dimensions	All W5s are used to create two or even multidimensional affinity charts, depicting the	The method is extremely useful for many *cost reduction* purposes and identifying 'bottlenecks', which equate to *improving throughput*

Continued

Analysis method/ type	Description	xBML dimensions used	Gain type
	For example, we may analyze *who* performs *what* work in a *Who × What affinity chart*. Or we may be interested in *who* uses *which* information (housed in which database), or *what* work occurs *when*, and so on	intersection points between any dimensions There are *over 80 potentially useful Affinity analyses* that can be performed! So the skill is knowing which ones to focus on, to yield the most gain	Affinity analyses can rapidly and visibly identify *duplication/ overlapping work*. They can rapidly and visually indicate where the same work is (redundantly) performed at multiple locations; where there is use of disparate or incorrect data sources; where the work is simply not being done, because no one is responsible; and much more . . .
3. Automation & IT enablement	A number of very advanced IT 'enablement' methods exist, all of which are far more sophisticated, detailed and accurate than anything available in the market (a strong but factual claim). A number of age-old problems are being solved with	All W5s and the *How* model	New opportunities for automation often result in *cost reduction of improved work throughout*; and *improved revenue* can also result. Of course, this assumes that the cost of automation is 'reasonable' and 'predictable'

potentially millions of dollars of savings/cost avoidance

Here are three ways to leverage xBML to better enable IT solutions: (i) automated business requirements generation – a unique capability exists to *auto-generated complete, consistent and virtually 'bullet-proof' business requirements* from xBML models – potential savings i.t.o. speed of production, completeness and accuracy are potentially enormous; (ii) COTS evaluation and implementation – *a discrete binary analysis* can be conducted against xBML models to 'scientifically' compare COTS solutions (for e.g. SAP®) to business needs; the delta (i.e. missing aspects in the software) can, for the first time, be *clearly identified*, as well as precisely mapped to the business in order to *understand business impact/change*; and (iii)

Automated, consistent and 'bullet-proof' business requirements, for the first time ever!

Say no more! Imagine if this statement were even half-true! (see later section devoted to this terribly important topic)

Our data suggest (after multiple SAP® 'recovery' projects) that many of the 'final few' experts are not only still living in the 20th century, but literally in the Dark Ages! The sorry stuff they produce (usually using a combination of Visio® charts and text) is outrageous, and this output has a very limited shelf life. Many myopic corporate leaders actually pay for this (it's in the 'final few''s

Continued

Analysis method/ type	Description	xBML dimensions used	Gain type
	system usage assessment/ rationalization – xBML can be used to map (in a discrete and binary manner) against existing systems and databases; in many instances, IT architectures have evolved into a tangled, messy web, essentially confusing the business and offering (multiple) disparate sources of data/information; a discrete binary mapping ability allows a complete picture of *who* uses *which* information, and *when* (and even *where*); officially sanctioned sources of data/information can then be selected, communicated and enforced		best interests to take as long as possible, after all their primary purpose is to maximize profits for their shareholders – and why not?) *Duplication* and *redundancy of corporate data* have reached epic proportions. It's a tangled web of confusion for most Fortune 500 corporations. A method that visibly depicts the use of data/ database/systems and helps clean up the tangled mess can potentially *save* an immense amount of *resources*

implement and manage them, are frankly appalling (we generalize, of course). Although this resourcing trend is extremely prevalent, it appears as if the decision is often made willy-nilly at the senior leadership level (often by analyzing macro costs) and a distinct lack of formal (micro) analysis exists. The motivation is often based on macro trends and industry 'peer pressure' or even, in some cases (arguably biased), business cases from outsourcing vendors.

In the instances that we are aware of where xBML has been used to support the evaluation of an (out)sourcing decision, the results were rather insightful. The business genetic xBML models identified many potential 'holes' in terms of missing activities (*what*) and *who* owned this work, and it also proactively forced the parties to better understand information sources and sharing (*which*). The methods also *proactively* revealed a number of new and critical activities (*what*), responsibilities (*who*) and information (*which*) that would be required (future state) to ensure the outsourcing arrangement actually worked.

(b) (Five-dimensional) business cost analysis (resource estimation)

By explicitly and completely describing the business genetically in five dimensions, xBML provides a foundational platform to estimate resource costs of a business model (typically a future-state model). This really is the '*how much*' question.

Traditional costing methodologies – e.g. Activity-based Costing (ABC) – have generally provided relatively high-level resource estimates (guesstimates) and largely ignored the dimensions other than activities (hence the name ABC) and *who* is performing these activities. **Metrics** can for the first time be associated – electronically if the **W5 software editor** is used – with each of the five business dimensions (and if necessary, at a very granular or detailed level).

Each of the W5 dimensions has a direct bearing on cost. Resource costs associated with the *What* and *Who* dimensions are fairly obvious. The *What* dimension addresses the cost of actually doing the work (the activity duration, of course, must be known). The major added benefit here is we can conduct the costing analysis at a macro level (perhaps levels 1 or 2 of the *What* model) or at a more detailed micro level (perhaps levels 5 or 6 of the *What* model).

Typically the more detailed the assessment (that is, the deeper one delves into the *What* model), the more accurately activity costs will be estimated. Further, we can also estimate the cost (perhaps for the first time) of *recursion* of activities (essentially redoing work) – in other words, how frequently do we perform the same activities in a given business domain? This is easily represented in the *How* model and, again, can be estimated at a macro or micro level, and down to individual transactions (e.g. install telephone service) level.

Since we have captured *who* is responsible for doing each of the activities, it is a simply a matter of attaching actual pay-scale data to each one on the *Who* model (electronically). This will give us specific insights as to the actual cost of performing business activities.

However, we are not done yet! So far, you can, hopefully, see that we are able to provide a more detailed ABC estimate to leadership. But each of the other dimensions may also significantly influence business costs;

- *Where*: the cost of performing business activities (*what*) in different geographies may greatly influence business costs; for example, the cost of doing work in Manhattan is very different to conducting the same task in Mumbai, India. Of course, this is the central premise behind outsourcing, and hence outsourcing analyses and cost analyses are very closely coupled.

- *When*: the frequency of performing tasks (*what*) will influence cost. Decisions may be made to perform certain activities less or more frequently, depending on how this influences cost. Or the converse may be true, it may be more cost effective to perform activities more frequently (say, validate client address information more often in order to ensure correct address information for each installation/truck roll).

- *Which*: the cost of gathering, storing, securing and maintaining information is often one of the most underestimated costs. Conducting certain business activities will usually require information (as discussed earlier) and these costs may be substantial. In one federal government xBML cost study, the *which* aspect (previously almost ignored) turned out to be one of the most significant cost factors, running into hundreds of millions of dollars.

Thus, xBML can provide a complete and detailed genetic picture of all the aspects and dimensions of a business that have a bearing on resource consumption or cost. This resource consumption/estimation data can be directly coupled to each of the W5 xBML genetic strands and electronically stored, retrieved and analyzed to provide a comprehensive estimate of the cost of doing business. Whether estimating a future (improved and rationalized) business state or determining where aspects of the business should be sourced, a W5 representation can provide a wealth of resource consumption estimation data to support business decisions.

(c)   Six Sigma and Lean Sigma revitalization

Finally, a number of corporations are vocally saying that Six Sigma and Lean Sigma desperately need some CPR! There is good news for our Six Sigma sect. In addition to the above analyses that can be performed against xBML models, an enlightened few of our Six Sigma/Lean colleagues have gotten pretty excited at the prospect of having *five data points* (W5, plus the *How* model) for Six Sigma/Lean analysis. And this, as opposed to a typical one- or two-dimensional and artistically crafted SIPOC (Supplier Inputs Process Outputs Customer) or Visio© chart. In fact, some have gone so far as to say that xBML may provide a much needed *revitalization* of their Six Sigma program. Since the low-hanging fruit has often been resoundingly plucked, some fresh business perspectives and insights might just be what Six Sigma/Lean needs? xBML can certainly provide a sound and scientific 'foundation' for the very decent and statistically centric Six Sigma analysis methods.

So yes, for any 'belts' reading this (probably both of you!), the slew of pretty robust and statistically/numerically based Six Sigma analysis methods can be very effectively used in conjunction with W5 genetic business models. xBML can become the definitive 'D' in DMAIC (Define Measure Analyze Improve Control). And what's more, this 'connectivity' can occur electronically (see the section on xBML automation, below). Additionally, xBML has proven useful in almost all (DMAIC) stages of the Six Sigma project. Box 6.1 illustrates the areas where xBML has been used by Six Sigma practitioners to directly support and supplement the DMAIC framework.

The net result is that xBML can certainly serve to rejuvenate Six Sigma or Lean initiatives. xBML and Six Sigma/Lean are *highly complementary*, they should never be viewed as 'competitive' (except by a myopic few), and to put it in the words of a master black belt practitioner, 'I now have Six Sigma on steroids!'

(d) Service-level agreement co-formulation/creation

There are a number of reports from organizations that have used xBML as the basis for Co-formulating (creating) Service-level agreements (SLA). The xBML foundation provides a wealth of business knowledge that can add a deal of clarity to SLAs.

Box 6.1   xBML support for Six Sigma DMAIC Framework

Define	Measure	Analyze	Improve	Control
• Identify process symptoms and validate with customers	• Define metrics for specific process areas (xBML)	• Evaluate and reduce variables	• Define possible solutions with corresponding operating tolerances (BCF, xBML)	• Determine ability to control (xBML)
• Map processes (BCF, xBML)	• Collect data for metrics	• Graphical analysis and hypothesis testing (xBML)	• Validate measurements for ongoing process monitoring (xBML)	• Implement process control systems (xBML)
• Identify process problems: causes, symptoms, outputs, non-value added work, non-standard work (xBML)	• Estimate process baseline capability (xBML)	• ID vital few factors (root causes) for process improvement (xBML)	• Plan process change (xBML)	
			• Implement process changes	

Essentially, an SLA specifies *who* will do *what*, and *when* and *where*. xBML specifies these dimensions in a visual format, but as you will see when we discuss the role of technology/software, it is a simple process to extract the xBML knowledge embedded in the symbology and represent this knowledge in a document or textual format. So, by means of a simple (electronic) *extract*, business knowledge regarding *who* is doing *what*, and *where* and *when* and with *which* information, can easily be exported and inserted into a (textual/Word®) SLA template/document (of your choice).

The added aspects to an SLA are business/SLA performance metrics associated with these business dimensions. Typically they define expected and agreed service levels or lead times. Well, all relevant metrics – in fact, any (and we literally mean any metric whatsoever – can easily be attached to any one of the W5 dimensions and electronically housed in the W5 editor software.[6] It really is a relatively easy process to store and extract this data and simply (electronically) generate the bulk of the SLA's content.

The results apparently have been very detailed. And major components of thorough SLAs covering many areas that normally were omitted, or not proactively even considered, have been electronically generated. So, to wrap this topic up, we have discussed some 'formal' approaches to leverage xBML business models to identify business Gain.

---

[6] This very powerful capability to electronically store absolutely any metric – about anything, in any format and of any size – and attach it to an xBML model is referred to as 'Profiling'.

You can see that there are many, many ways to use your genetic map of the business. The diversity is indeed surprising (even to the authors). It can help from supporting (out)sourcing initiatives to enhancing and revitalizing our Six Sigma capability. In many instances, new ways to leverage the knowledge embedded in the models (and, of course, the electronic xBML database) have come about due to innovation by clients and xBML practitioners. This has certainly fueled our enthusiasm and encouraged us to advocate many of the views expressed in this book.

The premise is: if you are truly able to map out a complete, accurate and consistent view of the business, then there is no need to use multiple different methods and tools to record different views (or sub-sets) of this business knowledge. *Model it once, model it right, and everyone can be on the same page and leverage the (foundational) output.* We will discuss this very important and potentially hugely beneficial topic later in this book. Also, all of the above applications or usages of xBML models have been well tested and fine-tuned with innumerable organizations. The result is *tangible, quantifiable and incremental business gain.* And remember, we have only discussed a sub-set of what is available!

6.2 Some more very real but less quantifiable types of business gain

It's all about the 'so what' factor, right? So, since we are trying to show value and introduce the notion of incremental or cumulative Gain, how can we further leverage these models for perhaps less quantifiable types of Gain?

In the previous section, we (rightly) emphasized *quantifiable Gain* but a reality check is needed here. There are many types of Gain that are often more difficult to quantify. They yield Gain but it is often difficult to relate these **less quantifiable Gains** ('blue dollar'[7]) directly to the income statement. Let's briefly look at a few of these very real but less tangible business Gains.

There are more 'blue dollar' applications of xBML than discussed here but, again, we will just focus on 'the top of the pops':

a. Keep me out of jail! (Regulatory compliance)

b. Industry standard '(blue)prints'

c. (Truly) understanding and communicating to others about your business

d. The aging workforce issue and institutionalizing business knowledge.

(a)   Keep me out of jail! (regulatory compliance)

Some factions in the federal government discovered, a few years back, that xBML was a very useful tool in helping to *understand massive regulatory complexity*. It turns out that

---

[7] Those gains that are not directly reflected on the income statement.

(ironically) the government has great difficulty interpreting the morass of complex and often contradictory laws it has created over the generations! Government also has increasingly great difficulty being compliant and allocating adequate budget to fulfill regulatory obligations. Frankly, it's a mess. And now, legislation is insidiously (and ubiquitously) infiltrating the private sector.

In the never-ending cycle of trying to secure constituents, more and more laws are being passed at a furious rate. Some with good intent but most with a big price tag, and one that directly and negatively affects our national (and global) productivity. And the problem is just getting worse and worse, with none of the prominent political parties apparently giving a hoot any more – that is, about anything other than winning the all too frequent political battles.

This massive legislative production machine (the biggest in the history of humankind!) is a significant contributor to 21st-century business complexity, with dozens of laws and counting (see Appendix C) affecting the average corporation. We urgently need management tools to help us understand this mess and ensure compliance (while being mindful of the cost implications), and, of course, keep our fine corporate citizens out of jail!

This ever-increasing legislative quagmire is something we all have to deal with, whether we are in the public or private sectors. Fortunately, laws and regulations are very easily 'translatable' using our newly introduced business genetic code or xBML methodology.

In fact, legislation's very purpose is to tell us what to do (*What*), albeit in a convoluted and verbose fashion. It is also applicable to specific geographies (*Where*) and usually identifies various legal entities, or parties (*Whos*) that are responsible. And laws usually reference time frames (*When*). So, laws and regulations in effect translate very neatly into our Who, What, Where, When and Which framework! The only missing piece is the *Which* informational aspect. Some legislation does, in fact, call out specific information requirements; and if not, it is usually a relatively simple process to derive the information needs (requirements) from the other dimensions.

But the real takeaway here is that xBML is an extremely useful tool to help business understand (in business or lay terms) what laws, accords and regulations call for. (Not to mention what a well-described/depicted process highlighting our financial controls can do for a dreaded Sarbanes-Oxley (SOX) compliance audit!) xBML can be used to simply translate, interpret and understand legislation. xBML will provide a simple graphic representation in a 'language' that mere mortals in the business community can readily understand (*sans* a Harvard or Oxford law degree).

xBML can also be used to assess existing (so-called *current-state*) business operations for compliance. It is a relatively simple affair to compare (in a discrete binary manner, that is a one-to-one mapping) a legal xBML model (a model that is literally translated (DCF'ed) from the law or regulation) with an xBML business model (a model BCF'ed with the business SMEs) and then determining whether what is called for by the

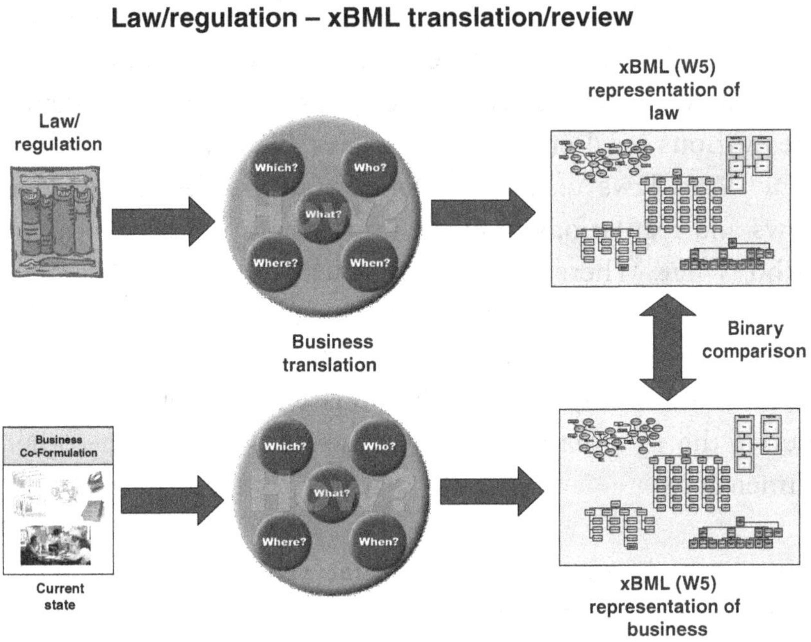

Law/regulation – xBML translation/review

Figure 6.3 Co-formulating laws and regulations in xBML.

regulation *is being done by the business*. QED, really. Figure 6.3 represents how xBML is used to compare laws/regulations against current-state business.

Here is a summary of laws, regulations and accords that we are aware of and that have been modeled in xBML (to a greater or lesser extent):

- BASEL II

- National Forest Management Act (NFMA)

- National Environment Protection Act (NEPA)

- Do Not Solicit (Colorado)

- Do Not Solicit (California)

- Health Insurance Portability and Accountability Act (HIPAA).

xBML can be used as an effective tool to help organizations better understand the impact of laws and regulations upon the business. In some instances, the Gain indeed has been quantitative (a major Telco avoided an estimated $30+ million in potential fines, as there were a number of exposures in their 'current-state' business model where they were out of compliance). In other instances, of course, it may be more difficult to assess the quantifiable Gain.

(b) Industry standard '(blue)prints'

Industry standard (blue)prints are somewhat similar in nature to laws, regulations and accords. 'Prints' can be easily represented in an xBML model and used to introduce industry 'best practices' to business operations in this structured and logical W5 framework. This has been done by a number of corporations.

At the time of publication, we are aware of a number of industry 'prints' that have been translated into xBML. Here is a list of some of the available xBML industry 'prints':

- ITOM (Information Technology Operating Model)

- ITIL (Information Technology Information Library)

- TOGAF (The Open Group Architecture Framework)

- SCOR (Supply-chain Operations Reference Model)

- NAM (Nuclear Asset Management Model)

- SNPM (Standard Nuclear Performance Model)

- AP913 (Nuclear-generation Equipment Reliability)

- Various industry-specific SAP® application 'prints'.

Note: Some of the above models are available from the parties that modeled them, standards bodies or from xBML Innovations, Inc.

For the record, it is worth noting most of the industry prints that have been translated into xBML have the following general characteristics:

- They are *incomplete*: they provide (as can be expected) one- or two-dimensional perspectives, usually focusing on activities, 'functions' and data.

- They lack necessary *detail and content*: all 'cut off' after a few levels of detail, and, unfortunately, that's where the devil or benefit lies!

- *Major gaps* and omissions exist: most of these prints are created in the absence of any formal methodological framework (like W5) and rely on 'art' or experience as the creation approach.

- Are housed in (*redundant*) 20th-century diagramming tools (or text): it is difficult to truly analyze or leverage 'pictures' (or text) that exist in image form only.

The takeaway here is that while these prints ensure some high-level consistency and standardization, they lack the completeness and necessary detail to be truly effective. As they say, 'all water looks drinkable at 10000ft'!

(c) (Truly) understanding and communicating to others about your business

You might be shocked to learn (or maybe not!) how many corporate leaders have confided that they truly *no longer understand what is going on in their organizations.*

If I only knew what my staff were doing, I am sure I could change the way we operate and be more effective and efficient as an organization. I am not sure why we have 12% more headcount than our closest competitor.

I have little faith in the financials that are produced and, consequently, have an entire team whose full-time job is to reconcile and validate, before we report earnings.

Scary quotes and both from a CFO of a $2.5 billion manufacturing company.

Leadership are, of course, aware (at some level) of what occurs in their organization but are often extremely frustrated, as they intuitively know things could operate more optimally. They are often powerless to guide their staff as to where and how to affect business improvements (hence the constant demand for consultants to solve the problem).

So, the first and foremost insight that will happen as a consequence of creating your genetic map or xBML model is plain and simple (diagrammatic) *understanding* of the business. Business professionals will rapidly (using BCF) obtain a *clear, concise and easy-to-understand picture (aka model) of the business*. And a lot of 'ah-ha's will spontaneously occur. This may well be the first time SMEs have ever seen a complete (multidimensional), detailed and clear representation of *how* the business actually operates!

Many of these 'spontaneous' or intuitive 'ah-ha's, are bona fide business improvements and often actually do *yield* some form of **quantifiable business gain**, albeit somewhat 'unscientifically'. In fact, one might argue that a large number of so-called business improvement projects (and certainly many consulting projects) are nothing more than engaging in dialogue about a business area, superficially mapping the process, and 'brainstorming' possible improvements with SMEs (remember TQM?), and, of course, usually led by the ubiquitous consultant.

But, in our case, a complete and detailed **W5 model** of the business is far more effective in guiding the SMEs through a logical foundation upon which to apply their collective expertise. The *Why* (do we do it this way?) question can be asked against this foundational understanding, and business improvements are more often than not forthcoming.

But do not underestimate the ability of your business SMEs. They generally know their business domain exceedingly well.

They have simply lacked a comprehensive visualization 'tool' to aid them through the process of understanding the proverbially big and complex picture of the world in which they operate.

In almost every instance of SMEs being exposed to a detailed and accurate xBML picture of the business, people can't but help identify improvements; for example:

The xBML Business Modeling Methodology is very executive-friendly. I was able to get full buy-in from our senior management with a 30 minute briefing of the methodology and output. Our subject matter experts (SMEs) were fully engaged when presented draft models the team created using the Document Co-Formulation process. The final resulting models were easy for executives and SMEs to understand and use for Business Process Improvement.
(Edward Henry, Strategic System Programs, US Navy)

We call these 'spontaneous' gains, identified by SMEs, **Quickwins** and staff are trained to capture (electronically embedded in the xBML models, of course) a 'profile' of these Quickwins, and where and how they 'touch' the business (model). Each Quickwin is usually assessed in terms of:

- Business impact

- Implementation effort and cost

- Time to implement

- (Quantifiable) Gain potential

- (Unquantifiable) Gain potential

- Net present value ROI.

Often these Quickwins are simply prioritized and approved by leadership, and then handed to a Project Manager or team leader for implementation.

Actually, the quantifiable gain of these Quickwins may well surprise you (they have often surprised us!). In fact, historically speaking, in almost every instance, Quickwins alone (without the more formal methods of analysis, discussed earlier in this chapter), more than justify the costs associated with training staff and building the business models! Really! We believe this is what the Americans call a 'no-brainer', right?

Almost always non-quantifiable business understanding will occur. It is gratifying to see the people who have created xBML models pasting them to office walls and making frequent reference to these visual 'genes' of the business.

If there are no Quickwins (highly unlikely!), you will nonetheless still be rewarded with a lucid, comprehensive and accurate understanding of the business, rest assured.

(d) The aging workforce issue and institutionalizing business knowledge

Another apparently looming crisis on the horizon is the retirement *en masse* of baby-boomers. The jury is still out as to the actual effects of this phenomenon. It is predicted by many that the *aging workforce* 'issue', and the corresponding lack of *institutionalized knowledge*, is large, looming and rapidly approaching. How, leaders ask, are we going to capture the vast quantities of knowledge that exist largely in the heads of the baby-boomers? *How do we rapidly harvest, assimilate, institutionalize and store this knowledge before they retire?* What tools exist to address this latent problem?

Well truly, not much! Yes, the 'final few' consultancies will conduct countless interviews (yet again) and neatly document (using text supported with Visio art) some knowledge for an outrageous (arguably non-justifiable) fee! But we now know that xBML models combined with knowledge harvesting methods like BCF/DCF can play a vital role in identifying and assimilating, and rapidly and productively capturing and even storing (electronically), this waning knowledge – in effect, institutionalizing this business knowledge.

The three compelling factors for using xBML here are:

1. Speed of knowledge harvesting/assimilation (particularly DCF).

2. Formal, complete and structured representation of business knowledge (the 5Ws).

3. (Electronic) storage/accessibility of this business knowledge in an 'open' database.

Indeed a powerful ally to address this emerging challenge.

For the record, a major multinational insurance group is using xBML to capture business knowledge, in order to ensure that relatively unskilled new hires are better equipped to understand the complexities of the corporation. This is a very effective way to ensure workforce development and education, using a consistent and pictorial representation of the business.

Of course, once these business models or genetic maps are created – regardless of the initial reason for their creation – they can be used for so much more than just storing business knowledge (remember?). As a by-product, you will have a true 'database' of (institutionalized) business knowledge to leverage for multiple initiatives! But more on that later.

Another aspect to note along the lines of understanding what is happening in your business is that an xBML representation will provide way more business insight than prior textual or 'informal' representations of knowledge. For instance, you will have five 'data points' or views of understanding, all electronically stored in a business database. These views can also be used to attach or embed various operational metrics[8] (again, another important topic that here we have only lightly touched on).

---

[8] In fact, after having worked with or for a number of Fortune 500 enterprises, one wonders how metrics, scorecards and corporate dashboards are really constructed, in the absence of a detailed understanding of all five dimensions of the business? Certainly many of the dashboards, metrics and scorecards we have seen are poorly thought through and lack insight into the inner workings of the business. They often measure the wrong thing or completely miss critical business insights (dimensions). Commonly such metrics focus on resource consumption and production and, consequently, can easily measure or focus on the wrong things – usually lagging rather than leading business indicators. This is something we have observed in very many corporations. We have encountered highly meaningful metric 'profiles' created by clients in the xBML Innovations W5 software that provide a valuable tool for better understanding, measuring and managing the business. These metric 'profiles' require a W5 business model as a solid foundation. Thereafter, meaningful metrics are defined and attached to one or more of the W5s, ensuring a meaningful connection to the business.

Most importantly of all, we have experientially found that business folk *actually use these models*, provided they are *aware* of them, *trained* to use them and have *access* to the technology.

To summarize, we have discussed that besides income statement improvement or quantifiable business Gain, xBML can also provide a reasonable non-quantified (passive) return on investment. We also discussed that 'informal' xBML business model reviews in most instances yield many actionable Qwickwins that often actually do yield quantifiable business gain. Many of these gains are difficult to quantify, but certainly make life much easier for people in the business. Additionally, we saw how business models can be used as a highly effective tool to understand *regulatory impacts* on your business, and discussed how xBML serves to rapidly capture and store a permanent *electronic record* of business knowledge – thereby effectively *institutionalizing this knowledge*. This can be used by anyone in the organization and will strongly support the looming aging workforce issue, or used to educate and inform staff about business operations.

Lastly, we mentioned how an xBML model can serve as a solid and complete foundation upon which to attach operational metrics and dashboards.

Indeed a lot to possibly leverage and there is still more!

7

How do
I implement this?

7.1   Enterprise deployment?

How do we implement and deploy this stuff? Well, *it depends*!

OK, so you didn't like that 'consultant speak'! So let's try and provide a simple but logical perspective. There is one fact that you will need to agree with: **approaching xBML deployment (or BPM, etc.) in an *ad hoc*, project-by-project fashion will ultimately result in a (much) more costly deployment**.

The cost associated with xBML deployment is represented in Figure 7.1. This graph illustrates the relative fiscal cost of deploying a programmatic BM capability versus an ad hoc project deployment.

Relative cumulative cost

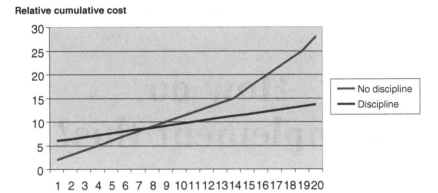

Figure 7.1 Programmatic and *ad hoc* xBML deployment *(courtesy: T. Hoekstra, The Sustainability Institute)*.

A *programmatic*, **or disciplined,** *deployment* is characterized by:

(a) *A* higher *upfont investment (cost)*.

(b) *Reuse of* xBML BM *output* (because of a consistent business definition methodology and associated infrastructure).

(c) *Increasing return/reducing cost* (as output is (re)leveraged across multiple initiatives and redefinition cost diminishes).

Conversely, an *ad hoc* **non-programmatic, non-disciplined, deployment** is characterized by:

(a) Low upfront investment (cost).

(b) Little (or no) reuse of project outputs (principally business models) i.e. output is used once, for the project at hand.

(c) Reducing return/increasing costs (as each project 'reinvests' in defining the business (problem) at hand).

The empirical data that professional firms like BusinessGenetics have accumulated clearly illustrate and support the cost-saving advantages of establishing an enterprise or programmatic capability, *provided that leadership have the fortitude to ensure that a 'critical mass' of projects actually leverage this infrastructure and investment.*

If not, then don't! Rather approach each project afresh. The cost threshold, to show an acceptable ROI, will be much higher on each project, because it is recognized that in many large organizations it may be very difficult (if not virtually impossible) to 'sell' (justify) an enterprise xBML BM capability.

There are tons of examples (a major Telco in Colorado, USA) where leadership are so panicked about any spend that operational leadership have quietly and effectively gone 'under the radar screen' and derived value on over 20 xBML projects! (Imagine what they could have accomplished with leadership support – talk about penny-wise, pound-foolish!)

The issue, of course, for a disciplined enterprise deployment is the upfront investment cost, and predicting the break-even point (and 'proving' it) – the very things that many corporations seem to have forgotten how to do. Or perhaps the current generation of corporate leadership (in general) appear to have lost the ability to invest for a quantifiable return? This is probably a result of the relentless cost reductions of late, and perhaps some of these leaders know of no other way. It's a shame, really.

Let us – in no uncertain terms (again) – make the point crystal clear (in case you missed it earlier): *A business strategy of relentless cost cutting is absolutely non-sustainable (in any commercial industry).*

In fairness, the hellatious investments and associated often pitiful return from many consultants/silver bullet trends has significantly contributed to the lack of confidence in large-scale enterprise changes. Let us also make it clear that this type of sophisticated 21CC solution does require some level of investment, based on over a dozen experiences of enterprise xBML BM deployment efforts.

Many deployments fall far short and reap only minimal (but still acceptable) returns. In some instances, companies incorrectly assume that by training a select few in the new approach (for a fraction of the required investment), 'magic' will suddenly occur. In contrast, some organizations approach their deployment from a larger enterprise competency center perspective and have *substantial and incremental returns* to show for their respective investments. OK, so just what kind of investment are we talking about? It really depends on many factors, including the size of the organization and organization process maturity level, to name just two factors. So, for your edification we have outlined a sample xBML *What* model of an enterprise deployment. This *What* model outlines the major activities that should or could be considered and/or undertaken in order to accomplish the purpose at hand (purposed-based thinking, remember?). Refer to Appendix D for a generic example which can be tailored or customized to your needs by your xBML BM deployment team.

Once you have identified *what* needs to be done to deploy an xBML capability, resource estimates can be attached to each task/activity. This should provide a useful framework for better understanding your deployment program and form a reasonable foundation for resource estimation.[1] The additional dimensions discussed in this book (*Who, When, Where, Which*) can also be added to complete the model.

Typically the bulk of the cost is in the training and certifying of personnel (not just the business modelers but SMEs, leadership and IT people and the business owners too). Additionally, the acquisition of software (especially enterprise software[2] enabling central storage, access and management of business models) may run into six (or even seven) figures.

To summarize, in the medium term, a programmatic, disciplined enterprise deployment will typically yield a greater ROI than an ad hoc *BM deployment. However, a programmatic deployment requires some form of upfront infrastructure investment, which may not be feasible. If this is not possible, all is not lost. Gains can be made on a project-by-project basis, although ROI will typically be lower (because of a higher total cost of investment, equating to the sum of reinvestment on all individual projects).*

---

[1] For the record, a full-blown cost estimator is embedded in the xBML Innovations W5 software tool.
[2] Please refer to Appendix F for a quick overview of xBML Automation.

7.2   But how do I implement or manage my xBML projects?

This topic may pose a bit of a quandary. (It is indeed a big topic and, as such, is earmarked for subsequent publications.) A sad reality is that even though you may choose to deploy a Business Genetic modeling capability in your organization, projects (believe it or not) may still fail. The mere fact that you can be equipped to map out the genetic code using xBML of your corporations will not necessarily guarantee a successful project. There are myriad factors that will influence the success of your business genetic mapping project, including:

(a) Project scope and duration

(b) Expected deliverables and output

(c) Project resources and budget

(d) Project milestones

(e) Impact on the business

(f) Leadership expectations

(g) The purpose of the project.

All these will influence the success of your project.

Indeed the 2004 Standish Group's CHAOS report, entitled *CHAOS Chronicles*, found that the total US IT project waste (albeit just IT projects), was over $140 billion, out of a total project spend of $255 billion in 2004. That is undeniably a staggering amount of waste and we are fearful that a very high percentage of BPR, process and BPM projects suffer the same (or worse!) fate.

So, this is indeed a perplexing dilemma. Even if we present the new BusinessGenetic code for understanding and improving business, the value is compromised by the absence of good project management. However, we have very good news. The gist of our solution, which will be elaborated elsewhere, follows very similar arguments to those presented in this book regarding the lack of formality and application of scientific rigor around business definition/depiction, but here directed at the project management fraternity. Despite eons of experience and the input of an overwhelming number of professional institutes, standards committees and certification, the sad fact is that just as we have lacked a formal method (language) to define/describe business, so too we have lacked *a formal method (language) to define/describe projects.*

Let's pause to contemplate this notion. There are tons and tons of **software tools** (*déjà vu*, eh?) to help the Project Manager, but again, many projects are run by 'do-ers' or those heroes that have a knack for getting stuff done. Software tools abound (especially the MS® Project®) and, of course, there is some good science to aid in analyzing project data (Critical Path Analysis, Earned Value Analysis, etc.), but little is available to aid in the actual *definition of the project*! (Is this sounding familiar, or what?) You may have made the intellectual leap. Yes, xBML can be used not only as a way to map out and describe the corporate genes, but also describe explicitly and completely all project activities. Projects consist of activities (*What*), performed by human resources (*Who*), at a place (*Where*) and in accordance with a schedule (*When*) that requires information (*Which*). So, the big conceptual leap is: **projects are foundationally (at the 'genetic' level) comprised of exactly the same five dimensions as any business.**

This is truly a conceptual leap, but for those that make it, it is quickly realized that: the *same xBML language (method) can simply be directed at any project* to create a robust, accurate, detailed and complete project definition of *Who*, is doing *What*, and *Where and When* and with *Which* information.

Although this notion may, at first, seem counter-intuitive, and even confusing, it is common practice for most xBML practitioners in the industry to begin each and every business (Improvement, Requirement Definition, Compliance, etc., etc.) initiative by first building an **xBML project model**. This xBML project model is used to define the schedule, estimate project resources (using the five-dimensional costing analysis discussed previously), scope the initiative, identify participants, determine project constraints, and so on, and usually exported (again, electronically) into a project management software tool (for example, Microsoft Project®) to manage project execution.

Let's use the example of a very simple Sarbanes-Oxley compliance project. We find there are *two* unique xBML models involved with this project. One is the actual business area mapping (for example, describing the current state operation

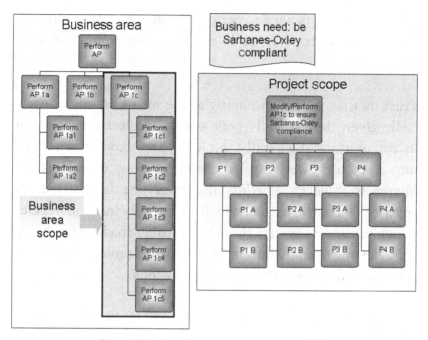

Figure 7.2 Creating xBML project models.

of, say, Accounts Payable), and the other is the project definition model. This latter model fully describes the project
purpose (ensure SOX compliance) and all the associated W5s
to fully describe the project. Note that only a high-level conceptual representation of the *What* models are provided in the
schematic in Figure 7.2.

In looking at the business *What* model, in Figure 7.2 you see
that the business area scope is that part of the business, we
want to be compliant with regulation – that is, 'Perform AP1c',
and the set of activities that supports the purpose of AP1c
(AP1a and AP1b) are not part of the business area scope.

The project *What* model, on the other hand (above right, in
the figure), defines those activities that the project team and

other stakeholders *need to perform* in order to ensure that the business area scope AP1c is modeled and compliant with Sarbanes-Oxley.

Trust us that we are chomping at the bit to say more, especially given the generally poor state of project management in corporations. Generally, project plans have degenerated into a set of PowerPoint® slides or, at best, the obligatory Microsoft Project® *schedule* that everyone largely ignores anyway. Of course, both of which are entirely inadequate. Our strong sentiment is that these are entirely inadequate, based on reviewing literally hundreds of so-called project plans from the best and brightest fortune corporations.

To summarize, the exact same xBML skill set that you acquire or create to conduct business modeling can be effectively deployed to (significantly) improve project management in your organization.

8

What about BPM (Business Process Management)?

WHAT IS THE BPM 'BUZZ' ALL ABOUT? IS IT IMPORTANT or yet another windmill to tilt at? Will this industry trend yield the results that BE and BPR failed to deliver?

Refer to the glossary to see the fairly diverse definitions that exist. David McCoy of Gartner offers the following definition:

BPM is a management practice that provides for governance of a business's process environment toward the goal of improving agility and operational performance. BPM is a structured approach employing methods, policies, metrics, management practices and software tools to manage and continuously optimize an organization's activities and processes.

McCoy readily admits BPM professionals have emphasized the 'process' part of BPM, overlooking the other two words 'business' and 'management'. But the 'process' part is absolutely the weakest link. In fact, the research we have conducted suggests that BPM is almost entirely software focused, albeit software to automate process.

BPM, or business process management as it is known by some of its suppliers/vendors, is largely centered around commercial off-the-shelf collections of (highly configurable) software which supports the automation and monitoring of specific business processes. Its origin is largely from workflow companies and document imaging companies, although some IT design vendors have rapidly repackaged and positioned their software to exploit this trend.

Business process/Performance management and/or Monitoring and/or Service-oriented architecture (SOA) promises process management nirvana – namely, the ability to (rapidly and inexpensively) automate, manage and monitor all (key) 'processes' in the business.

Now, that's a proverbial big deal, especially given the fact that automating anything at all (no matter how trivial)[1] from a business perspective has apparently become as complicated as getting through airport security with a nail-clipper. Why so? The industry long ago abandoned the notion of IT/system application architectures – the net result being a software

---

[1] A senior leader in a major office products company admitted that the business had long ago 'given up' on most system improvement requests, based on the unfortunate fact that the improvement request queue numbered in the thousands.

application architectural disaster. Data/information and applications are randomly scattered across the enterprise, duplicated, triplicated, x-licated and forever unsynchronized. It is an unfortunate catastrophe.

But architectural disasters aside, is there any hope? Can we possibly 'superimpose' process oversight software (Uberware) which will automate, manage, monitor and interface with our legacy environment? Truly, a miracle cure!

All, good questions. The analysts and event organizers are promoting this new trend something fierce. And that's both good and bad. What's bad is that, as mentioned previously, almost everyone is working from the incorrect assumption that we know *how* to define a 'process' or business. Vendors, academics and business leaders are all working from 'process' definitions that have the consistency of cold, lumpy porridge. It's not pretty.

A case in point is that one of the leading BPM software solutions (and we are talking north of $5 million in implementation costs) is having the devil of a time showing clients any tangible ROI. The major issue then, with the BPM software in question, is the decidedly 20th-century 'process' definitions used by this product. Indeed, they exhibit all of the characteristics of 'junk science' mentioned earlier in this book:

1. **A two-dimensional focus**: defining (at best) a sub-set of activities and responsibilities.

2. **Incomplete or missing critical business information (dimensions)**: enough said!

3. **Level mixing**: absence of checks and balances (rule set) to avoid mixing 'high-level' and 'lower-level' business activities – resulting in disparity in the 'model'.

4. **Dumbed-down process definitions**: employed, perhaps, in an attempt to 'get through' the process definition as quickly as possible (ensuring that business SMEs are at least somewhat engaged), with input process definitions so high level as to be almost completely useless (all water, for instance, looks drinkable at 50 000 ft). Come on, we are talking enormous 21st-century business complexity which may consist of an extremely complex choreography of hundreds or thousands of multidimensional components (the 5Ws) and we attempt to define these 'processes' with a simplistic 'stream-of-conscious' string of activities (usually 20–30)!

5. **Junk science (Art)**: the 'gotcha' for those that create these 'process' definitions is what governs what goes inside the boxes. Perhaps anything that 'feels' right or looks intuitively OK? And, of course, the 'skill' can't be replicated.

6. **Poor (or no) theoretical foundation**: the 'process' definition is still at the 'collection of activities' level and way too vague to be much good at all.

7. **Limited (or no) analytical/business improvement capability**: we are in the midst of the 'technological revolution' and still do not have the ability to create and use a structured database of our business knowledge. Technology provides a significant opportunity electronically to store, under-

stand, communicate, analyze, slice-and-dice and report on, etc. all manner of information about the business. The question is how can we *not* be using such technology?

8. **Limited (or no) reuse**: these 'process' definitions are, again, created with a single (often disposable) use. Reusing these business definitions, no matter how crude and artistic, is most often *not even a consideration*!

9. **Unproductive knowledge harvesting**: little or no thought is given to leveraging existing knowledge sources of business definition/depiction. Most of the time it's a classic and very costly 'wheel reinvention'.

Now, we are the first to admit that many BPM software tools are sexy, with abundant flashing-light alerts, great API with existing legacy databases and applications, super graphics and GUI, etc., but it is a classic case of garbage in, garbage out! Of course, your BPM software can work, should you be lucky enough to possess a 'process' definition Van Gogh, who can 'intuitively' describe massive complexity while keeping the business SMEs totally engaged! The point here is these puppies are sold on their 'noble features'. So, it is most often a struggle to justify such software products based on debatable ROI.

However, solidify the business definitions and these products can truly 'sing', for the fact is *that without a formal, robust definition of the business (way beyond 'process'), BPM will simply not fly.*

BPM does indeed hold much promise. Software that can automate the business, alert us to potential business issues in advance, etc., is very, very appealing. Such software can help alleviate the quagmire that has evolved because of an ever-decreasing de-emphasis on 'formal' architectures (application, data and business architectures primarily). Additionally, BPM can finally provide a useful 'architecture' of knowledge and software tools to produce a variety of valuable aids to both the business and information technologist. Some of the benefits of such a BPM 'architecture' include:

(a) Providing a *business-friendly IT front end* (GUI) to the business.

(b) Providing a central 'place' (repository) to *store business and application meta-data.*

(c) Providing a *robust business knowledge store/interface platform* to leverage other technologies and software.

This being a hot new market, it has attracted the attention of the standards bodies. The BP standards groups have defined a useful 'architectural framework' for the BPM-enabled corporation. There are also multiple (unfortunately) evolving standards which impact the functionality and capabilities of BPM software. These standards include those from the object management group (OMG), and the workflow management coalition (WFMC), to name but two.

Lastly, by looking at the acronym that is BPM, we need to focus for a minute on the 'M'. As stated above, M stands for management. In the classical Demmingesque definition, to manage means to plan, organize, execute and monitor. The current focus of BPM software is on the *monitoring* part of the definition. As such, it is critical to develop metrics that are organizationally and strategically aligned and can be meaningfully applied to the BPM system. You need, therefore, to develop metrics using a holistic view of the organization, which can be explicitly connected to the detailed processes that are automated by the BPM software. There is a need to model at 50 000 ft (where all water appears drinkable) as well as at the 2-ft level, to provide a meaningful framework for the business model and associated metrics.

The key takeaway here is, before investing in fairly costly BPM software, to make sure you have the capability (preferably in-house) to adequately and robustly *define the business (processes)*.

Dumbing down enormous business complexity in order to 'bang in' a BPM tool, just because it is punted by vendors and industry experts, is *not* a sound strategy. And as we said earlier, *a fool with a tool is usually a bigger fool!*

To conclude, for us to realize the full (and promising) potential of BPM, it is absolutely critical we significantly improve our base definition/depiction of the so-called business 'process'. Absolutely everything hinges on a sound, complete and formal representation thereof. Without revisiting the fundamentals (i.e. how do we robustly define/depict a business), BPM will fall sort of the hyperbole and most probably simply 'morph' into some new trend.

9

What the heck is the difference between BPEL, BPMN, UML, IDEF and xBML?

To understand these differences, we'll look at the original intent of each of the languages, depiction techniques or notation techniques, and provide examples of each. This is not meant to be an exhaustive comparison of these respective approaches and methods, rather it is meant to provide a succinct overview of the more popular techniques and methods in use today.

We think the best way to frame this discussion, is by defining the steps or actions that we believe are necessary to build a model of a business or operation. These are a sub-set of the methods that are included in a complete discipline of business modeling.

In order to build a model of a business or operation, you need to:

1. Capture the business information from all knowledge sources.

2. Organize the business information into meaningful constructs.

3. Validate that the business information is complete and consistent.

4. Communicate the business information among the stakeholders.

We will use this set of steps to compare the following techniques, methods and languages.

9.1 BPEL

The business process execution language (BPEL) was invented to allow an XML-based *communication* between software products that closely support workflow automation. As such, its usefulness as a means of human communication is limited, if not completely unsuitable. In fact, by looking at the example below, we think it is self-evident that BPEL is not suitable for the capture, organization, validation or communication of business information to business people:

```xml
<?xml version="1.0" encoding="utf-8"?>

<process name="insuranceSelectionProcess"
    targetNamespace="http://packtpub.com/bpel/example/"
    xmlns="http://schemas.xmlsoap.org/ws/2003/03/business-
process/"
    xmlns:ins="http://packtpub.com/bpel/insurance/"
    xmlns:com="http://packtpub.com/bpel/company/" >

  <partnerLinks>
    <partnerLink name="client"
      partnerLinkType="com:selectionLT"
      myRole="insuranceSelectionService"/>

    <partnerLink name="insuranceA"
      partnerLinkType="ins:insuranceLT"
      myRole="insuranceRequester"
      partnerRole="insuranceService"/>

    <partnerLink name="insuranceB"
      partnerLinkType="ins:insuranceLT"
      myRole="insuranceRequester"
      partnerRole="insuranceService"/>

  </partnerLinks>

  <variables>
    <!- input for BPEL process ->
    <variable name="InsuranceRequest"
      messageType="ins:InsuranceRequestMessage"/>
    <!- output from insurance A ->
    <variable name="InsuranceAResposne"
      messageType="ins:InsuranceResponseMessage"/>
    <!- output from insurance B ->
    <variable name="InsuranceBResposne"
      messageType="ins:InsuranceResponseMessage"/>
    <!- output from BPEL process ->
    <variable name="InsuranceSelectionResponse"
      messageType="ins:InsuranceResponseMessage"/>

  </variables>

  <sequence>
```

```
<!- Receive the initial request from client ->
<receive partnerLink="client"
   portType="com:InsuranceSelectionPT"
   operation="SelectInsurance"
   variable="InsuranceRequest"
   createInstance="yes" />


<!- Make concurrent invocations to Insurance A and B ->
<flow>

  <!- Invoke Insurance A web service ->
  <invoke partnerLink="insuranceA"
    portType="ins:ComputeInsurancePremiumPT"
    operation="ComputeInsurancePremium"
    inputVariable="InsuranceRequest"
    outputVariable="InsuranceAResposne" />


<!- Invoke Insurance B web service ->
<invoke partnerLink="insuranceB"
   portType="ins:ComputeInsurancePremiumPT"
   operation="ComputeInsurancePremium"
   inputVariable="InsuranceRequest"
   outputVariable="InsuranceBResposne" />


</flow>

<!- Select the best offer and construct the response ->
<switch>

  <case condition="bpws:getVariableData('InsuranceAResposne',
                'confirmationData','/confirmationData/Amount')
             <= bpws:getVariableData('InsuranceBResposne',

'confirmationData','/confirmationData/Amount')">

     <!- Select Insurance A ->
     <assign>
       <copy>
         <from variable="InsuranceAResposne" />
         <to variable="InsuranceSelectionResponse"/>
       </copy>
     </assign>
   </case>
```

```
    <otherwise>
     <!- Select Insurance B ->
     <assign>
      <copy>
        <from variable="InsuranceBResposne" />
        <to variable="InsuranceSelectionResponse"/>
      </copy>
     </assign>
    </otherwise>
   </switch>

     <!- Send a response to the client ->
     <reply partnerLink="client"
        portType="com:InsuranceSelectionPT"
        operation="SelectInsurance"
        variable="InsuranceSelectionResponse"/>

   </sequence>

</process>
```

As a means to communicate between BPM software tools and applications, BPEL is indeed a very powerful tool. BPEL, then, provides us with *a simple, powerful mechanism to transfer data about the business between applications.* Period.

Some mistakenly presume BPEL to be a definition or modeling language. This is clearly not the case. It is strictly a 'language of communication', and a formal methodology for understanding, defining and capturing business knowledge is clearly a prerequisite to using a communication language like BPEL.

The BPEL taxonomy cannot distinguish between a 'good' or 'bad' business definition, and it is as effective in communicating foundationally flawed or detailed tapestries of the business.

9.2 BPMN

Business Process Modeling Notation (BPMN) was invented to make BPEL more easily understood by humans. That said, the documentation for BPMN states:

The primary goal of BPMN is to provide a notation that is readily understandable by all business users, from the business analysts that create the initial drafts of the processes, to the technical developers responsible for implementing the technology that will perform those processes, and finally, to the business people who will manage and monitor those processes. Thus, BPMN creates a standardized bridge for the gap between the business process design and process implementation.

In some ways, it has moved from what is the completely artistic and 'ad hoc art form' of flow modeling toward a proposed standardized set of icons or symbology.

It does nothing, however, to address some of the primary issues with flow modeling – for instance, defining explicitly what an activity is (i.e. what goes in the box), or the arbitrary and 'unrepresentative' real-world constraints of sequential or time-based modeling. This means that the primary manner or technique for associating the activities a business performs in BPMN is linear, time-based and sequential. This is fine for most workflow-based processes, especially those that you might want to automate with a workflow engine. Nevertheless, it is no more applicable to the current complex and chronologically interrelated environments in which today's businesses operate than any other flow modeling technique. (We should note, however, that there is a concept or construct of an '*ad hoc* process' contained within BPMN. This construct allows for the grouping of activities without sequence but there is no relationship syntax defined to connect the activities.)

In terms of defining an activity, BPMN does nothing except to say that it is a 'generic term for work the company performs':

An activity can be atomic or non-atomic (compound). The types of activities that are a part of a process model are: process, sub-process and task. Tasks and sub-processes are rounded rectangles. Processes are either unbounded or are contained within a Pool.

This definition does little to guide the BPMN practitioner in determining what type of information goes in the activity box. That is, there are no rules to guide the practitioner in the definition or identification of a bona fida activity; not to mention the fact that there is no discernment between a process, sub-process, task or activity. All rather confusing, really.

Additionally, BPMN suffers from being too technical, exemplified by the fact that there are *over 50 graphical icons* required to be understood by business users. And the icons have a technical or automation basis for their existence. For example, if you look at the definition in the event type called 'Cancel', this is what you will find:

This type of end is used within a Transaction sub-process. It will indicate that the Transaction should be cancelled and will trigger a Cancel intermediate event attached to the sub-process boundary. In addition, it will indicate that a Transaction protocol cancel message should be sent to any entities involved in the transaction.

Just try to get leadership, process owner or an accounts payable clerk to understand that!

The techno-centric nature of BPMN is also exemplified by the fact that it is directly translatable into BPEL. One might also note that the great vast majority of the contributing authors to the standard are technology suppliers/vendors. Go figure!

Finally, we need to, again, emphasize that BPMN is primarily a *depiction technique for information (albeit constrained and limited) about a process*. There is little, if any, guidance regarding which information about the business to capture, and how to ensure whether that information is complete and consistent.

As such, BPMN is no more suited than classical 20th-century workflow modeling (discussed earlier) to support the capture, organization and validation steps of business process modeling.

Figures 9.1 and 9.2 present two BPMN examples. Upon closer inspection of these examples, we find them fraught with issues. For example, the use of 'anything' in a box – in the first example (Figure 9.1) you see no structure to the content of the activity boxes. We see the term 'Review issue list' fol-

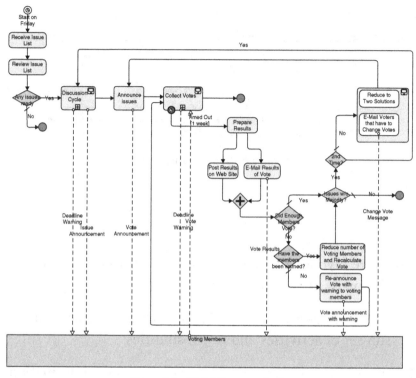

Figure 9.1 BPMN example 1.

lowed by 'Discussion cycle'. Now, the former is reasonably clear as an activity but the questions you might ask are: who reviews the activity, what information is contained in the issue list and where is this review done and, finally, when is this review done? In looking at 'Discussion cycle', you might simply ask what the dickens the term means?

In the second example (Figure 9.2), there are clearly steps missing, but exactly what is missing? While it's a little unfair to take this diagram out of context, it does exemplify the free-form nature of the BPMN specification.

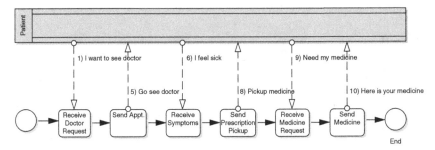

Figure 9.2 BPMN example 2.

There are myriad other unresolved issues associated with this anachronistic approach; for instance:

1. A one- or two-dimensional focus, defining at best only a sub-set of activities and responsibilities.

2. Incomplete or missing critical business information (dimensions).

3. Level mixing, without checks and balances (rule set) to avoid the mixing of 'high-level' and 'lower-level' business activities, and resulting in disparity in the 'model'. In fact, it's far more complex. With the artificial notion of processes, sub-processes, tasks and activities, all with minimal (or at best vague) definitional rules, we have a proverbial dog's breakfast. And this is just one dimension of the business (the *What*)!

4. Dumbed-down process definitions, by nature of the approach. In the absence of a structured, hierarchical foundational notation, this approach does not support detailed (complex) business definition.

5. Inadequate definition rules, where the 'gotcha' for those who create these 'process' definitions is what governs what goes inside the boxes. Perhaps anything that 'feels' right or looks intuitively OK? And, of course, the 'talent' employed in creating the model can't be replicated.

6. A poor or no theoretical foundation, where the process definition is still at the 'collection of activities' level. This is way too vague to be of much use.

In summary, BPMN does little to facilitate business understanding and is fraught with all the issues of classical process flow modeling.

9.3 UML

The unified modeling language (UML) was originally invented as a way to describe and design object-oriented computer software; and it was subsequently enhanced to be used as the requirements gathering technique to support object-oriented design. As such, it has constructs, syntax and components more suited to object-oriented design and development than describing how a business operates. This original intent has not hampered the misuse of what is a great software design technique to describe business process and operations.

This entire approach is based on the somewhat academic notion that the systems (and natural) world consists of 'objects'. These objects, once identified, can be classified into types and then structured. Objects essentially equate to

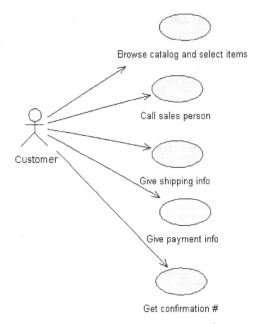

Browse catalog and select items

Call sales person

Customer

Give shipping info

Give payment info

Get confirmation #

Figure 9.3 UML use case example.

'nouns' in the business. As previously mentioned, attempting to identify all the (business) objects in even a simple business domain is the most frustrating, time-consuming, futile, unproductive and wasteful experience we can recall! In fact, it is almost impossible to engage anyone from the business in the tedious and tiresome exercise. Of course, the approach works exceedingly well in the IT arena, and one can see how the UML constructs may aid IT folk.

Each UML diagram is designed to let developers and customers view a software system from a different perspective and in varying degrees of abstraction (see examples of commonly created visual modeling tools in Figures 9.3–9.9).

The *use case* diagram (Figure 9.3) displays the relationship among actors and use cases. *Class diagrams* model

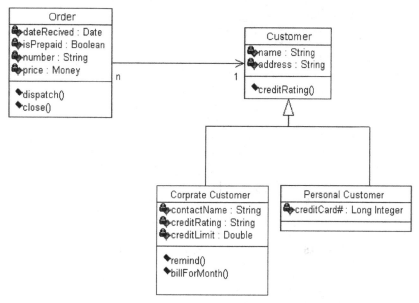

Figure 9.4 UML object class diagram example.

class structure and contents, using design elements such as classes, packages and objects. They also display relationships such as containment, inheritance, associations and others (Figure 9.4).

Interaction diagrams depict the following (Figures 9.5 and 9.6):

- The sequence diagram displays the time sequence of the objects participating in the interaction. This consists of the vertical dimension (time) and horizontal dimension (different objects).

- The collaboration diagram displays an interaction organized around the objects and their links to one another. Numbers are used to show the sequence of messages.

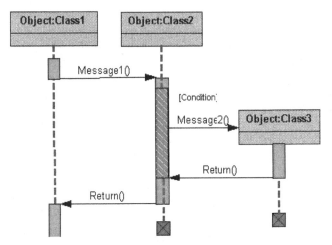

Figure 9.5 UML object sequence diagram example.

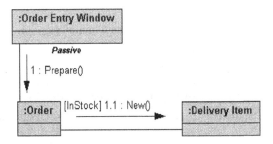

Figure 9.6 UML object collaboration diagram example.

State diagrams display the sequences of states that an object of an interaction goes through during its life in response to received stimuli, together with its responses and actions (Figure 9.7).

Activity diagrams display a special state diagram where most of the states are action states, and most of the transitions are triggered by completion of the actions in the source states. This diagram focuses on flows driven by internal processing (Figure 9.8).

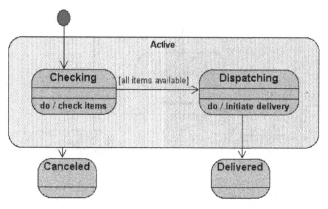

Figure 9.7 UML object state diagram example.

Physical diagrams depict the following (Figure 9.9):

- The component diagram displays the high-level packaged structure of the code itself. Dependencies among components are shown, including source code components, binary code components, and executable components. Some components exist at compile time, at link time and at run times, as well as at more than one time.

- The deployment diagram displays the configuration of run-time processing elements and the software components, processes and objects that live on them. Software component instances represent run-time manifestations of code units.

In practice, only two of these diagrams are widely used to describe business. The first is the activity diagram and the second is the use case diagram.

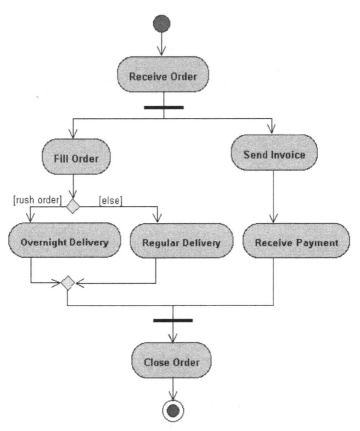

Figure 9.8 UML object activity diagram example.

The activity diagram is really just a flow diagram and therefore provides little more guidance on the syntax of what goes into a box than any of the other flow methods. This means, that UML provides no guidance as to what business information the practitioner needs to gather, nor, once information is gathered, how the practitioner should organize it to ensure completeness and consistency.

The use case provides an association between business activities, system capabilities, information and actors (or people).

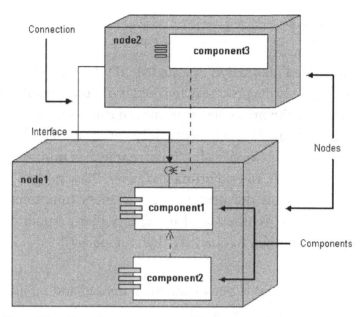

Figure 9.9 UML object component/deployment diagram example.

So, it is useful for understanding the capabilities of the software system in supporting specific business activities. However, this does little in aiding the business person to understand, validate and communicate the business process; it also assumes that it is a simple matter to define and identify the activities and actors!

In summary, UML provides little benefit over artistic workflow modeling, in terms of helping the business understanding itself. If truth be told, this approach, while having merit in the IT arena, has limited use for business modeling. It is exceedingly confusing to business representatives, is technocentric and based on 'theory' that is far removed from business operations.

9.4 IDEF

The integrated definition method(s) (IDEF) was originally invented to describe processes for the USAF. It is arguably the most fit of all the preceding examples in this section to do so (although marginally). Unfortunately, even though its use spans in excess of two decades, its acceptance is minimal. We believe this is due to two primary reasons. The method principally focuses on the depiction of business functions and data. The major Achilles' heel is the fact that a 'function' is even more nebulous to quantify than an 'object'!

The term 'function' is one of the most abused and misunderstood terms around. Certainly, it promotes ambiguity, and in practice mixes 'processes, activities and organization units' with gay abandon – essentially confusing the heck out of business representatives! The method then, in mind-numbing detail, focuses on identifying and defining data entities and attributes. Ironically, the theory used is sound and rooted in mathematics (functional dependency theory); but usually this massive overkill places it way out of the domain of business modeling. Additionally, the method abstracts key information about the business; and specifically, the use of mechanisms and controls are poorly understood and difficult for many business users to understand.

Secondly, IDEF is a depiction method and contains no supporting methods for information gathering or capture and minimal syntactical checks for the information contained in the models. So while it is more 'scientific' than the average run-of-the-mill flowchart, it is not ideal (or even sufficient) to

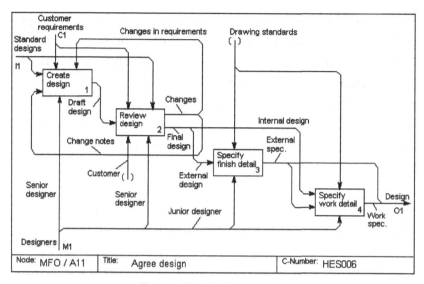

Figure 9.10 IDEF example.

allow simple, consistent understanding and description of a business process. Figure 9.10 presents an example where the function/flow diagram represents a slight improvement on the more informal Visio® mapping techniques that abound. No wonder, perhaps, deployments of this approach are few and far between.

9.5 xBML

Lastly, let's again summarily contrast xBML to some of the perspectives discussed above. The extended business modeling language was created to provide a rapid yet complete, rigorous and repeatable set of methods that allows anyone in any organization to describe and communicate – explicitly, yet simply – their business operations.

The extended business modeling language was invented specifically to describe the genetic or atomic components found in every business. After years of research, we have empirically proven that there are a total of five pieces of information necessary to describe the operation of an organization. These components are easily understood by everyone in an organization and the resultant model can be verified algorithmically as being complete and consistent.

Again, the primary dimensions of the extended business modeling language are: What does the business do (activity), Who does the activity, Where is the activity done, When is the activity done, and Which information is consumed or produced by the activity? These dimensions, as we call them, are everyday ideas and concepts ('objects', if you will) used by everyone in the business or organization.

For each of these dimensions there is a specific syntax, which enables the practitioner to know *exactly* what to put in the 'box'. Additionally, there are *rules* that specifically guide the practitioner on how to organize the business information and to ensure the completeness thereof. These features ensure the speed, simplicity and accuracy of xBML business models. Finally, a sequence of activities is used only when necessary to support communication to humans or downstream automation. Activities (in their natural state) are grouped and organized based on their *business purpose* – a far more stable, simple and meaningful structure than one based on time or sequence. What xBML does is to provide a rapid, yet complete, rigorous and repeatable set of methods, and these enable anyone in the organization to describe and communicate – explicitly, yet simply – their operations. This can also be applied at various levels of complexity, from the viewpoint of high-level leadership down to that of the minutiae of operations.

Let's, again, quickly look at just one of the xBML models, namely the *What* model, and take the 'Discussion cycle' activity from the BPMN model. Using xBML, we take the box 'Discussion cycle', which contains no active verb, and prefix it with active 'perform' (this is one of the rules of xBML, that is 'an activity must consist of an active verb and a qualified object'). Using this newly minted activity, we ask: 'What do you need to do in order to perform a discussion cycle?' In asking that question, we may come up with a model, as follows.

If we 'Post the issue in a new thread', 'Determine the issue discussion time frame', 'Identify the voting members', 'Notify the voting members of the new thread' or 'Notify the voting members of the issue discussion time frame', then we have performed a discussion cycle. This may also be turned into a completeness question, such as: 'If I post the issue in a new thread, determine the thread discussion time frame, identify the voting members, notify the voting members of the new thread and notify the voting member of the issue discussion time frame, have I performed a discussion cycle? Yes or no?' But only a binary response is allowed in this xBML model (see Figure 9.11).

While this is not a completely rationalized *What* model, we have provided explicit meaning for the term 'Perform discussion cycle', and an explicit and complete set of activities to support the capture of the additional business information,

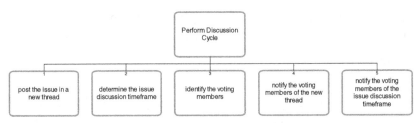

Figure 9.11 xBML *What* model example.

namely: who does the activity and what information is consumed or produced by the activity, and where and when is the activity done?

We also provided a framework to ask questions like: 'What do we do in order to identify the voting members?', 'What do we do in order to notify the voting members?', 'Who are the voting members?', 'What is an issue discussion time frame?' The answer to all of these questions adds to the explicit business-centered understanding of the activity 'Perform discussion cycle'.

While the information required to answer these questions may come from any knowledge source – whether explicit, implicit or tacit – the xBML framework contains specific methods that allow the practitioner to know what information to capture, and how to organize it, and ensure its completeness and communicate it.

We have not looked at all the models in xBML. As previously discussed there is a specific model for each of the **W5** dimensions: *What, Who, When, Where* and *Which*, as well as a sequence model called the *How* (W5I) model. Each additional model augments the capture, organization, validation and communication features discussed in this section.

In summary, the above has given the reader insight into some of the varying techniques available and in use today for describing business operations. You should be able to see, as a result of this brief overview, that many of the techniques are flow-based depiction techniques that come from a technical origin. As such, they are most appropriately used when the practitioner is commutating business processes that are naturally sequential. In general, they offer little or no guidance regarding what business information to capture, how to organize it, or validate its' completeness and consistency. However, none provides as robust a framework for the capture, organization, validation and communication of business information as xBML.

10

Based on (anticipated) popular demand, more on auto-business requirements generation

Getting IT to automate what businesses really want, and getting the businesses to clearly describe what they really want, are quests for the Holy Grail.

Frankly, the state of the 'Enterprise Divide'[1] in corporations is as bad as ever. Or more correctly, worse than ever (particularly in the United States). It seems that, in this field, IT

---

[1] The division that has classically existed between IT departments and the business. IT rarely delivers IT solutions that satisfy the demands of the business, and conversely, the business is ill-equipped with methods and tools to clearly articulate what it is that they *require* to be automated.

qualifications, corporate and academic standards and the state-of-the-science, have reached an all-time nadir that is very concerning.

The *'free spirited, non-standardized, trust us, short-term focused, we can't afford standards/architecture, focus on cool technology, experienced folks are too expensive, killer app savior, what's discipline?, Jack Bauer hero mentality, outsource it, fire the CIO every 2 years* mentality and characteristics of the IT 'profession' *should be a major cause for serious concern.* How on earth do we bridge the 'enterprise divide' which apparently is fast becoming a chasm?

Well, believe it or not, and as mentioned earlier, once a W5 business model has been created, amazing things in IT can (and should) occur. Of course, you will probably have to first replace the existing 'gen X guard', who no doubt still believe that chronically naive 'use cases' or 'user stories' (giggle) or better yet, a newer (even more rapid) SDLC (exploratory prototyping, in essence), has a hope in heck of addressing the issue, and that the business actually gives a darn!)

The fact of the matter is that absolutely astounding results have been achieved by IT people using xBML models. And we do mean *astounding*. For a start, our researchers and advanced practitioners have shown that creating usable Business Requirements, the age-old industry pariah, has been *solved*. Yes, solved! Period.

Certain organizations are using xBML models and xBMLi software to 'auto-magically' (ha-ha) generate robust (dare we say, 'bullet-proof') *business requirements*. We have indeed implied that Business Requirement Documents (BRDs) can be automatically generated from xBML models. At least a dozen pioneers (some of whom were on the initial 'bleeding edge') have used xBML to automatically extract robust business requirements, and Gartner® have written a case study on the remarkable success achieved at Pitney Bowes on this front.

This means that once an xBML model has been created (for business improvement, regulatory compliance, etc.), *the same xBML model can also be used to generate business requirements*. (Note a recurring and important message here!) This is illustrated in Figure 10.1.

No additional (or at worst, minimal) effort is required: no separate IT-driven project to endlessly interview 'users', no expensive consultants or contractors, no user stories or use(less) case definition, etc. Zero, nada, zip. Just a complete **xBML model** and the **xBMLi Business Requirements extraction software**. Period.

Zounds, it sounds too good to be true! Well, it's a reality, and this approach is now used as a standard at one of the largest banks in the US, at one of the largest mail service company in the world, and many others. Pay attention to this capability: let's repeat it one more time. *The age-old problem of creating usable business requirements is finally solved.* An xBML model can be used to **automatically create a robust set of business requirements**, with minimal effort. (This may be reason enough to pay closer attention to even the preceding chapters!)

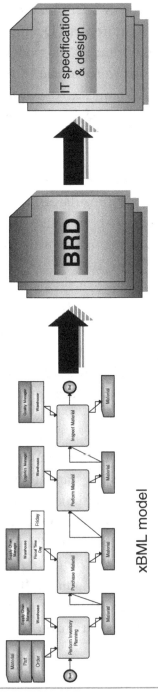

xBML model

Figure 10.1 xBML automated business requirement generation.

This may indeed sound a little 'out there', but think about it for an instant. If we can genuinely genetically describe business consistently, accurately and completely as we have discussed, and store this knowledge about the business in a structured, consistent (electronic) format (i.e. a database), then it is a relatively simple proposition to 'transform', 'manipulate' and extract the (business) data about how the business operates (or more correctly, what the business requires to be automated), to a format that easily exceeds anything the industry has ever seen before. It really is that simple.

We apologize for repeating this, but it has been our unfortunate experience to find that most IT folk (especially CIOs) simply don't believe this is possible. For these flat-earthers, please heed Arthur C. Clarke's 'Third Law': 'Any sufficiently advanced technology is indistinguishable from magic' (Arthur C. Clarke, 1961).

We challenge you to 'inventory' the current method and associated output for business requirements generation in your organization. Odds are definitely strongly in our favor, that at best a hodgepodge of less than useful (textual) 'templates' exist (usually in Excel® spreadsheets) and the business is pretty much expected to 'fill in the blanks' (random streams or snippets of consciousness, really), sometimes with the aid of a totally business illiterate from IT, or perhaps worse, a consultant.

The business 'knowledge' gathering methodology usually consists of interviews or workshops, with vague question like: 'What do you want the system to do?', or a largely business-unfriendly use case or ultra naive user story. Come on, no wonder the Standish Reports cite IT project success at a lowly 21% (imagine if we had this type of project 'success' in other disciplines such as building, engineering, medical, etc.).

The proverbial (Six Sigma) 'root-cause analysis' points firmly to the lack of halfway decent business requirements as the primary cause of IT project failure (validated by the Standish Report on software development success statistics). Ludicrous isn't it? But why is it so?

Let's share a little-known insider secret here. (We can sense many 'experts' already getting super-defensive!) But here it is: *no one really knows what a business requirement actually is*. Seriously!

Again, let's use our 'define a business' ploy and ask them to define 'a business requirement'. (Sit back, enjoy and listen to the nebulous waffle that will emanate! It's cruel, really!) To illustrate the point, here is a definition of a business requirement from an industry 'expert': 'What you want or desire from a system, which you believe will deliver a business advantage.' (Oh boy, I thought our old definition of process was nebulous.)

The industry pundits and academics in the 'requirements' field have lost their way. Business requirement methods that do exist are so IT or software tool centered that they are pretty much useless to the business. And we ironically call them *business* requirements! In fact, many business requirement gathering work sessions alienate the business as they are so counter-intuitive and technocentric.

In reality, the rest of these business requirement software tool are glorified spreadsheets that assume (or encourage) requirements to be captured in Dark Age 'textual' format, derived from random streams-of-consciousness from business professionals corralled into 'requirement workshops', who will blurt out anything that will get them off the hook! Any excuse to get out, even a root canal seems more palatable!

So, we reiterate one last time: very robust business requirements can be *automatically generated, in a repeatable, consistent and structured manner, directly from xBML models.* This is indeed a huge leap forward and some industry lieutenants have adopted xBML simply for this reason. The plain truth is that, if this claim is accurate, then you really do not have any other viable alternative to gather business requirements.

A sample Business Requirement Template Document, which can be generated (without human touch), from the xBML Innovations software can be found in Appendix D. Also included is a table indicating all the potential content that can be extracted from an xBML model and included into a BRD.

11

COTS (commercial-off-the shelf) software selection

I F xBML CAN BE USED TO CREATE BUSINESS REQUIREMENTS, what about selecting commercial off-the-shelf software applications – for example, ERP (enterprise resource planning) systems (SAP, Oracle, Great Plains, etc.), and CRM (customer relationship management) systems (Siebel, Sales Force, etc.)? In addition, there are industry-specific and function-specific COTS software too numerous to mention. As we all know, a gaggle of horror stories exist, describing package software implementations. These include being six years into a four-month implementation, stopping the implementation after five times the original time and budget and rolling out the system – only to hear the cries of the users as they attempt to do what they have done for the past 20 years in a new, convoluted and inefficient manner.

As with most application software projects, the root cause of implementation challenges lies in two areas. The first of these is classic poor business requirements that have been identified for the past two decades as one of the top reasons software projects fail. The second reason is more specifically allied to COTS software. It lies in the hidden or unidentified costs not anticipated in the implementation. Many of these unidentified costs can be mitigated by using the software vendors' predetermined implementation plan; however, the ones that are not anticipated are related to *failure to understand the business impact* prior to implementation.

Specifically, organizations need to avoid 'automating the cow path' – that is, do not automate bad business practices. The software will enable you to conduct bad business at a much faster rate than before!

It is recommended that the business domains are mapped out and understood as the first logical step to COTS deployment. Thereafter, the very same business models should be used for improvement of the business. And lastly, the very same models should be used for business requirements generation. Can xBML be used as the basis for this approach? Heck, yes.

In an xBML-based COTS selection, the methodology can be used to:

(a) model the implementation project

(b) model the business area

(c) improve the business area

(d) generate the requirements

(e) generate the test scripts for user acceptance testing.

This suggested approach mitigates the inherent risks typically found in COTS selection projects and aligns business transformation with the technological capabilities of the COTS software.

xBML's innate ability to utilize a single model for both business improvement as well as business requirements, together with its ability to model projects, make it a unique and efficient approach to COTS selection projects.

12

An added big, big takeaway

O K, CONGRATULATIONS. YOU HAVE READ THIS FAR AND presumably 'got it'! Here is an added (mega?) bonus. We hope you can take significant advantage of this concept, which is uniquely enabled if you deploy xBML.

We have alluded to this a number of times in this book. It's the notion of **massive and broad-scale reuse of business models**. Think about this for a moment. How many initiatives are running right now in your organization? Probably dozens, if not hundreds, for most Fortune 500 organizations. They may include:

- business improvement

- multiple IT projects

- Six Sigma or Lean efforts

- Sarbanes-Oxley

- BASEL II compliance (for banks)

- Regulatory compliance

- BPM

- Workflow

- Content management

- Corporate dashboards/scorecard

- The next merger or acquisition

- The latest business area that's to be 're-sourced', etc.

Now contemplate what each and every one of the above corporate initiatives do first . . . Surprise, surprise, they all start by *describing or depicting the business area at hand!* Let's test this briefly.

Business improvement efforts definitely start by 'mapping out the business process' (albeit with junk science and a blank canvas!). IT projects always start by defining business requirements (again, an art form comparable to early cave-dwellers' renderings). Six Sigma's DMAIC (Define, Measure, Analyze, Improve and Control) absolutely states that one of the first steps is 'Define the business/process'; and Sarbanes-Oxley (Section 404) direct us to 'document our financial controls'.

Most regulatory forms require us to 'show' compliance, hence describing our business (process) is essential.

One of the first steps pre-/post-merger is to align core organization functions and processes (financial reporting, accounting, HR 'processes', etc.), so some form of assessment/definition and comparison of the business is required. And, of course, most have now learned that to willy-nilly outsource and trust that your outsourcing partner takes care of things is as ludicrous as assuming the major airline executives have a strategy other than seeing how badly they can annoy customers! So, the more you understand (describe/depict) the business area to be outsourced, the better.

The above shows that everyone is relentlessly (and in splendid isolation) describing the business! And doing it very differently! Again and again, and yet again! At what outrageous cost? Why? Well, perhaps because we have lacked a complete, detailed and formal method of describing our business? Or we have such disparate and poor business definitions that other project team members can't make sense of them? Or both?

If we had such a capability to describe the business (once) completely, maybe, just maybe, *we can genetically describe (model) the business once and leverage the business model relentlessly!* This notion is depicted in Figure 12.1. We dare you to calculate the resources that all of the initiatives have consumed in the upfront 'define/understand the business'

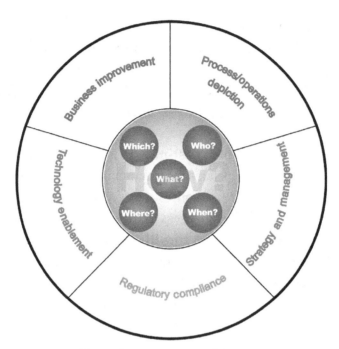

Figure 12.1 Business model reuse.

phase. You know, it is staggering. IT consumes, how much resource each year on Business Requirements definition (not to mention the cost of the SMEs and contractors/consultants involved in this process)? What about all that business defini- tion done by the Sarbanes-Oxley team (and we haven't even got to the Business Improvement and Six Sigma yet)! It has to be tens of millions per year for a sizable Fortune 500 company, right? And that's just per year. Imagine the (quantum) savings if you did define/depict the business once and every initiative leveraged the same models (Box 12.1).

If you have the capability to model the business completely, consistently and accurately once, you can shamelessly lever- age these definitions for almost all major corporate initia- tives. However, this can only be accomplished if you have a

---

Box 12.1   Business modeling waste due to no model reuse

Assume 20 sizable business initiatives/projects of the types mentioned above. Assume that, on average, each initiative deploys 10 resources for five elapsed months (or 50 effort months). That conservatively equates to 1000 effort months. Let's assume just the labor costs (no loading, overhead or consultants – again, conservatively speaking) are around $10000. That equates to a whopping $10000000 (for any given year!)

Even if these numbers are off, say, by a factor of 25%, just extrapolate the potential gain in productivity in your corporation over five years.

Now take this concept to the national level. Image such savings for all Fortune 500 organizations. That equates to a staggering $5000000000/year!

'common language' for genetically describing/depicting the business that all can learn and understand and have access to. The potential savings can be enormous!

And one final point: yes once a model is built, it will need to be updated periodically to reflect business changes. Our experience shows us that the effort to (briefly) update a business model to reflect business changes is significantly and substantially less than starting from a blank canvas (see the earlier discussion on the merits of DCF).

13

A quick last summary

WE BEGAN BY SAYING THE INDUSTRY LACKED SOUND methods and tools for truly understanding the 'business' and how it operates. We also noted that we lack a sound theory of what a business really consists of.

In the early chapters, we discussed how 20th-century business definitions and theory are rather nebulous and general in nature. Existing academic and theoretical contributions have consisted of high-level concepts or frameworks, for example: 'people, process and technology, activity strings, objects' and the like. These concepts do not enable a very detailed of insightful understanding of a business. These definitions and concepts often inhibit us from truly understanding a corporation's genetic makeup, at a detailed level. And they certainly fall far short in aiding the understand of the intricate and complex choreography that makes up the 21st-century corporation. Worst of all, such concepts and frameworks are not supported by any supplemental 'scientific' definition theory. Consequently, any resultant business definition is largely based on the 'artistic' merits and experience of the business-modeling practitioner. There is no 'rule set' to test or ascertain whether these definitions are reflective of the business reality that they attempt to represent/depict.

So not only do we lack good theoretical frameworks to understand our 21st-century corporations, we lack rule sets to validate our business definitions.

We have also reflected that if our tools are lacking, this is a major obstacle to conducting commerce in the 21st century. We summarized the very challenging characteristics of 21CC and concluded that 21CC is set to become even more complex. We provided some fundamental new thoughts and tools for understanding 21CC.

Our notion of a genetic blueprint for understanding the business is based on an intuitive framework that addresses a given business purpose (*why*), *who* does *what* work, and with *which* information, and *where* and *when* it is done. We called this genetic framework the W5s. This gave us a sound platform upon which to base our genetic map or description/definition of the business. Thereafter, we introduced the notion of using a *set of formal rules* (that almost anyone can learn) that *facilitate the answering of the W5 questions.*

This is the world first, and most critics and process 'flat-earthers', unfortunately, entirely miss this point. Frameworks may exist, but the leap forward here is *the ability to answer the questions using a repeatable and consistent rule set that yields repeatable output, as opposed to artistry.*

We have also illustrated that by answering the W5 questions with the rules (akin to grammar and hence a *language* of business definition), we can create a set of easy to understand *business-facing* pictures or models (genetic blueprints). Thereby we create a five-dimensional set of all that knowledge that any business person may need to truly understand the organization (or sub-set thereof). We discussed how this xBML definition is literally a major leap ahead of most 20th-century business definitions, depiction approaches and tools. It can bring an entirely new and detailed understanding of our complex business operations.

Creating this multidimensional definition can be done in a fraction of the time traditionally taken, for we now have advanced capabilities that can leverage (recycle) existing knowledge stores (business artifacts). This only becomes possible because we have introduced a *common denominator* that provides a complete foundation for our business. Gone are the tiresome (and costly) days of running lengthy, one-on-one unproductive work sessions with business representatives (not to mention the dark days of 'interviewing' all and sundry).

Equipped with our new set of Business Genetic tools, we can understand business like never before, and it is now possible to conduct formal (and informal) analyses against our 'database' of structured business knowledge. We briefly categorized here the most popular types of improvement and shared the most common analysis methods. Further, besides using xBML models for formal analysis, a host of methods and informal techniques exist that can add much value to the corporation, in a non-quantifiable way.

xBML can be deployed on an *ad hoc* basis or in a programmatic fashion (competency center). The merits of these approaches have been discussed, together with the ability to use our W5 approach to define projects – projects of every type. Exactly the same knowledge that is acquired in mapping out the business can be applied to the world of Project Management.

We highlighted that the current BPM trend should take note of the demise of BPR and BPI. It is our belief that a serious flaw exists in the inability to accurately, comprehensively and repeatedly describe the business. One can logically conclude that, if you can't describe business, you certainly can't improve, re-engineer or automate it. The same is of course true for all information technology and process improvement initiatives.

Finally, we have tried to convince you to reuse your **business genetic maps and business definitions**. Do not, we repeat, *do not*, treat these valuable business models as disposable commodities. They are *indispensable corporate assets* that truly map out your **corporate DNA. Define once and reuse relentlessly** must become our corporate mantra. The potential upside is enormous. We urge you to consider the productivity gains of this concept at your corporation. Pretty cool, huh?

So the conclusion is that there are huge (even gargantuan) bottom-line impacts to be had by foundationally rethinking the way we understand and describe business. There are gains from explicitly and consistently understanding your business. There are gains from the efficient and effective reuse of the plethora of business documentation that already exists. And finally, there are immense gains from the reuse of the explicit genetic business xBML models as the foundation or starting point of all corporate initiatives. Every bit of this, and more is easily within your grasp by simply joining the Business Genetics revolution. See you there!!

Appendices

Appendix A: xBML example – 'Fill a vacant job position'

The *What* model.

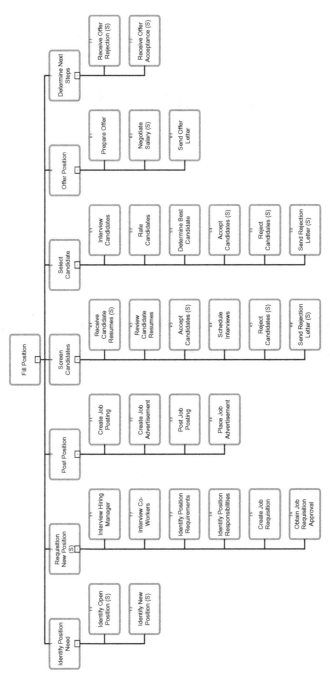

Figure A.1 *What* model example.

The *Who* model.

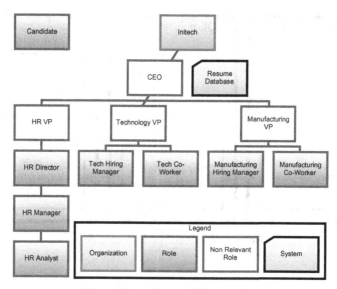

Figure A.2 *Who* model example.

The *Where* model.

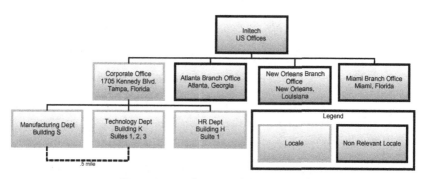

Figure A.3 *Where* model example.

The *When* model.

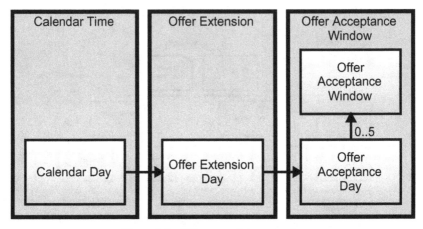

Figure A.4 *When* model example.

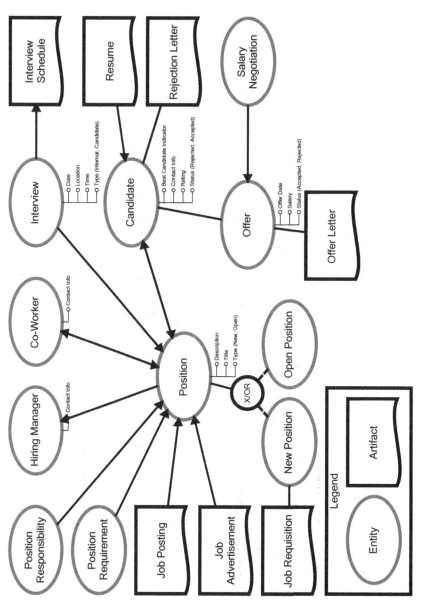

Figure A.5 *Which* model example.

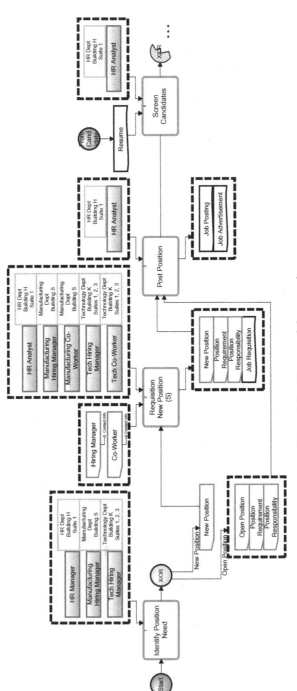

Figure A.6 *How* model example.

Appendix B: Potential knowledge sources

Examples of sources of knowledge/artifacts

Following are examples of documentation artifacts and other sources of knowledge used to describe business operations. One or many of these may be available for use during Document Co-Formulation™:

- Business plans
- Business cases
- Strategy documents
- Contracts
- Organizational charts
- Job descriptions
- Work instructions
- User manuals
- Directories
- Legal court documents
- Financial reports

- Statements of work
- Personal binders
- Value chains
- Flowcharts
- Websites
- System flow diagrams
- Process maps
- IT architectures
- Application code
- Workflow diagrams
- Network diagrams

- Audits
- Meeting minutes
- Policies

- Trouble ticket logs
- UML-based use cases
- Databases

Typical source documentation formats

- Microsoft Excel worksheets
- Microsoft Word documents
- Adobe Acrobat documents
- Email communications

- Microsoft Visio drawings
- Microsoft PowerPoint presentations
- Text documents
- Screen shots

Appendix C: Some government laws governing commerce

Schedule A: Federal Department of Labor laws

- <u>Wages and hours of work</u>

  - Minimum Wage and Overtime Pay

  - Wage Garnishment

- Migrant and Seasonal Agricultural Worker Protection

- Child Labor (Nonagricultural Work)

- **Safety and health standards**

  - Occupational Safety and Health

  - Mine Safety and Health

  - Migrant and Seasonal Agricultural Worker Protection

  - Child Labor (Nonagricultural Work)

- **Health benefits and retirement standards**

  - Employee Benefit Plans

  - Black Lung Compensation

  - Longshore and Harbor Workers' Compensation

- **Other workplace standards**

  - Family and Medical Leave

  - Lie Detector Tests

  - Whistleblower Protection

  - Plant Closings and Mass Layoffs

- – Union Members

- – Uniformed Service Members

- **Work authorization for non-US citizens**

  - – Authorized Workers

  - – Temporary Agricultural Workers (H-2A Visas)

  - – Temporary Nonagricultural Workers (H-2B Visas)

  - – Workers in Professional and Specialty Occupations (H-1B Visas)

  - – Permanent Employment of Workers Based on Immigration

  - – Nurses (H-1C Visas)

  - – Crewmembers (D-1 Visas)

- **Federal contracts: wages, hours of work and fringe benefits**

  - – Wages in Supply and Equipment Contracts

  - – Prevailing Wages in Service Contracts

  - – Prevailing Wages in Construction Contracts

  - – Hours and Safety Standards in Construction Contracts

- "Kickbacks" in Federally Funded Construction (Cope-land Act)

- **Federal contracts: equal opportunity**

  - Employment Discrimination and Equal Opportunity in Supply and Service Contracts (Executive Order 11246)

  - Employment Discrimination in Construction Contracts (Executive Order 11246)

  - Equal Opportunity for Individuals with Disabilities

  - Employment Discrimination and Equal Opportunity for Certain Veterans Who Served on Active Duty and Special Disabled Veterans

- **Index of Acts by Specific Industry**

  - **Agriculture**

    - Fair Labor Standards Act (FLSA)

    - Migrant and Seasonal Agricultural Worker Protection Act (MSPA)

    - Occupational Safety and Health Act (OSH Act)

    - Authorized Workers (Non-U.S. Citizens)

    - Temporary Agricultural Workers (H-2A Visas)

- **Immigration and Nationality Act (INA) 1994**

  - Section A

  - Section B

  - Section C

- **Mining**

  - Federal Mine Safety and Health Act of 1977

  - Black Lung Compensation

- **Construction**

  - Occupational Safety and Health Act (OSH Act)

  - Davis-Bacon Act and Related Acts

  - Copeland Act ("Kickbacks" in Federally Funded Construction)

  - Executive Order 11246 (Employment Discrimination in Construction Contracts)

    >> Section A

    >> Section B

- **Transportation**

  - Occupational Safety and Health Act (OSH Act)

Schedule B: National Environment Protection Agency laws

More than a dozen major statutes or laws form the legal basis for the programs of the Environmental Protection Agency (EPA).

- **National Environmental Policy Act (NEPA) 1969**; 42 U.S.C. 4321–4347. NEPA is the basic national charter for protection of the environment. It establishes policy, sets goals and provides means for carrying out the policy.

- **Chemical Safety Information, Site Security and Fuels Regulatory Relief Act 1999**; Public Law 106–140, January 6, 1999; 42 U.S.C. 7412(r)
  Amendment to Section 112(r) of the Clean Air Act.

- **Clean Air Act (CAA) 1970**; 42 U.S.C. s/s 7401 *et seq.*

- **Clean Water Act (CWA) 1977**; 33 U.S.C. s/s1251 *et seq.*

- **Comprehensive Environmental Response, Compensation and Liability Act (CERCLA or Superfund) 1980**; 42 U.S.C. s/s 9601 *et seq.*

- **Emergency Planning and Community Right-to-Know Act (EPCRA) 1986**; 42 U.S.C. 11011 *et seq.*

- **Endangered Species Act (ESA) 1973**; 7 U.S.C. 136;16 U.S.C. 460 *et seq.*

- Federal Insecticide, Fungicide and Rodenticide Act (FIFRA) **1972**; 7 U.S.C. s/s 135 *et seq.*

- Federal Food, Drugs and Cosmetic Act (FFDCA) **1906**; 21 U.S.C. 301 *et seq.*

- Food Quality Protection Act (FQPA) **1996**; Public Law 104–170, August 3, 1996.

- Freedom of Information Act (FOIA) **1966**; U.S.C. s/s 552.

- Occupational Safety and Health Act (OSHA) **1970**; 29 U.S.C. 651 *et seq.*

- Oil Pollution Act (OPA) **1990**; 33 U.S.C. 2702–2761.

- Pollution Prevention Act (PPA) **1990**; 42 U.S.C. 13101 and 13102, s/s *et seq.*

- Resource Conservation and Recovery Act (RCRA) **1976**; 42 U.S.C. s/s 321 *et seq.*

- Safe Drinking Water Act (SDWA) **1974**; 42 U.S.C. s/s 300f *et seq.*

- Superfund Amendments and Reauthorization Act (SARA) **1986**; 42 U.S.C. 9601 *et seq.*

- Toxic Substances Control Act (TSCA) **1976**; 15 U.S.C. s/s 2601 *et seq.*

Appendix D: Sample Enterprise Deployment *What* model

The Enterprise Deployment *What* model (Figure A.7).

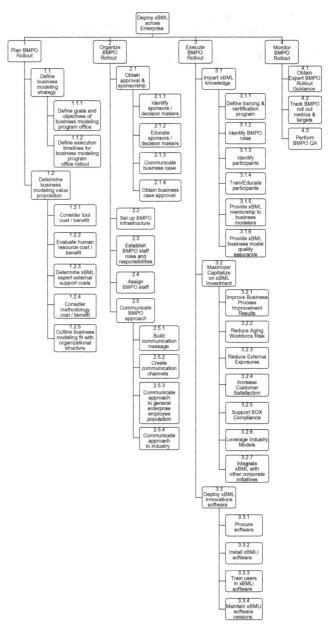

Figure A.7 xBML *What* deployment model.

Appendix E: BRD

xBML Business Requirement Document (BRD) template: potential content

1. BRD title and reference information

2. Activities to be automated

3. Data requirements

4. Use cases

5. Workflows and decision logic

6. Security and access requirements

7. Maintenance routines and APIs

8. Reporting requirements

9. Temporal trigger requirements

10. Network topography requirements

11. Business terms glossary.

Table E.1

#	Requirement sub-set	xBML dimension used to derive requirement	Requirement document format	Value to IT	Suggested requirement document heading	Added value requirements
1.	Provide a list of all business activities that the business wants automated	What model	Indented list of activities and (sub)children	Denotes all candidate activities for automation; these can be compared to existing system/COTS functionality or translated into technical program designs (using Jackson or Garfunkel PSD methods)	Business activities Required to be automated	Prioritize each activity 1–5 (grading from 'Mission critical' to 'Nice to have')
2.	Provide an access matrix for each activity (*What*), indicating who will perform the activity	*Who* (extended), *What* and *How* (additional 'system access' *Who*-level input will need to be obtained)	Matrix	Provides a detailed understanding of security requirements, indicating who, at a detailed level, will execute the activity on the system, and who will need to be able to perform the activity	Who will perform the automated activities	

3.	Provide a list of all business information requirements	*Which*	Indented list (entities and associated attributes)	Provides a detailed list of all the business entities (objects and events) that the business needs to be stored in a database; for each entity all associated attributes must also be listed, showing details that the business requires to be stored for each entity; and this requirement will form the foundation for creating the data schema or configuring/ refining existing schemas	Information that is required to be stored/accessed	Business criticality of having this information stored electronically can be denoted; possible values (or ranges) of attributes can be denoted
4.	Provide a list of all *Which* model assertions	*Which*	Entities and associated textual assertions	Provides a business foundation for creating data schemas and maintenance rules	Rules we require to be applied to stored information	
5.	Provide a list of data usage (consumption/ production)	*How*	Data Inputs: Activity:Data Outputs	Provides a view of the activities that create, update, produce or delete information;	Information inputs and output requirements	Can attach CRUD indicators

Continued

Requirement sub-set	xBML dimension used to derive requirement	Requirement document format	Value to IT	Suggested requirement document heading	Added value requirements
6. Provide input regarding information access and security	*Which, How, Who*	Matrix	Defines who will have access to which information and how they will use the information (CRUD)	Security and information access requirements	
7. Provide maintenance routine requirements	*Which, What, How*	Indented list	Defines all maintenance routines required, as well as applicable business rules	Maintenance requirements	Prioritize each requirement 1–5 (grading from 'Mission critical' to 'Nice to have')
8. Provide transaction processing requirements	*Which, What, How*	Indented list	Defines all maintenance routines required, as well as applicable business rules	Transaction requirements	Prioritize each requirement 1–5 (grading from 'Mission critical' to 'Nice to have')
9. Provide use cases	*Who, Which, What*	*Who, What, Which*	Creates use cases	Use case requirements	Existing databases/ systems can be depicted

10. Provide temporal triggers	*What, When How*	*When, What*	Identifies the time governance associated to business activities (i.e. *when* does each *what* temporally occur)	When are required activities to be executed/ performed	Sequential activities (i.e. those not governed by explicit time frames can also be denoted/included)
11. Provide geographic need	*What, Where*	*Where, What*	Defines the business activities that will be performed/required at each geographic location	Where we require activities to be performed	
12. List external interaction points	*How*	List	Identifies the external interactions/connections to other systems/ processes	External system interactions	
13. Indicate reporting requirements	*Which, What*	List	List the reporting requirements	Reporting requirements	Can create report/ screen 'paints' (mock-ups)
14. List glossary of terms	*Which*	Summarized list	Clarifies business terminology	Business terminology glossary	Should be an appendix

Appendix F: Can xBML be automated?

It would be fabulous indeed if all the knowledge about the business was accessible electronically by everyone across the enterprise. Even better, wouldn't it be grand if all the various factions/initiatives could import this business knowledge into other electronic tools; for example, IT database design tools, Six Sigma analysis tools, Sarbanes-Oxley repositories, IT requirement managers, etc.?

In fact, this is not a desired state, it's an absolute necessity. The severe limitations of many 20th-century business depiction tools are that most are merely *depiction tools*. That is, they do not store business knowledge in a structured and accessible format: there is no database. To say the least, this is a severe constraint. Unfortunately, some tools that do indeed store business knowledge (usually a sub-set thereof) in a structured electronic format (database) are rendered proprietary and, hence, inaccessible to the very folk that need this critical knowledge! Thus, the reuse of business (process) models, is effectively prohibited or certainly restricted.

21st-century technology provides the exceedingly powerful ability to house, store, manipulate, view and leverage this foundational information about the business. Any software tool that lacks this capability should be discarded as having little to offer the business. Not only should technology allow the structured storage and access to critical business knowledge, but provide a 'business knowledge architecture' (see Figure A.8). The schematic in the figure indicates the following capabilities are required for any robust business modeling 'suite':

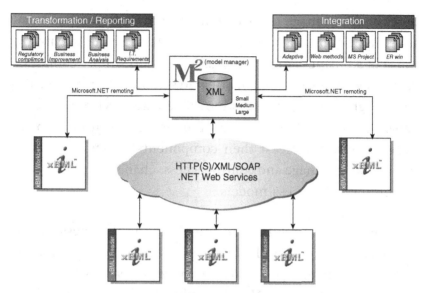

Figure A.8 xBML BPM architecture *(courtesy: xBML Innovations)*.

- Capturing and editing business models

- Enforcing business model methodology rules

- Reading and viewing business models

- Importing business models

- Exporting business models

- Analyzing business models

- Reporting business knowledge

- Managing business knowledge

- Web-enabling business knowledge

Software to manage the creation, storage and access to business models is an absolute necessity. In fact, the rewards of reuse of a business model (discussed earlier) simply cannot be realized without fairly sophisticated software that will ensure the integrity of all business models created. Without such a capability, the potential for overlap and duplication of business models (or at least their components) exists. Such software should manage and control access, changes and additions to enterprise business models.

A robust software suite will allow all this business (meta) knowledge about how the business operates, to be electronically stored in an 'open' and accessible database. xBML Innovations uses tagged XML (eXtensible Markup Language), so like any database, this business knowledge can be:

- *Shared*

- *Viewed*

- *Queried*

- *Analyzed*

- *Managed and controlled (access and security)*

- *Sliced and diced*

- *Reported upon*

- *Interfaced and used by other software tools (for e.g. process automation, business requirement management, business analysis, Six Sigma, project management, etc.).*

Lastly, all business models must be housed in an open and accessible database (repository), preferably in XML format. Beware of any 'closed' or proprietary databases. These are very limiting, and frankly, they are not in touch with the sophisticated technology of today.

Providing a means for clear communications is important enough, but xBML is also a powerful 'front-end' to XML, the *lingua franca* of the computer industry. The translation from xBML to XML is simple and straightforward and opens a world of possibilities, from instant compatibility with thousands of existing systems to direct translation into computer programs and databases. Another equally easy and powerful translation is from xBML to UML, an important standard in the area of system design. These two relationships provide the ability to express a business need only once, and then to use the appropriate translation to turn the statement of need into system and information designs.

Glossary

21CC

21st-century Commerce, a term used to describe the complexity of conducting business in the 21st century.

ABC

Activity-based Costing, traditional method of estimating the cost of a business domain, using business activities as a foundation.

AP913

An equipment reliability process description established by the Institute of Nuclear Power Operations (INPO).

BCF

Business Co-Formulation, technique for rapidly gathering unstructured business information and synthesizing this knowledge into a meaningful and coherent framework.

BM

Business Modeling, the discipline of representing a business in an orderly, schematic manner.

BPEL

Business Process Execution Language was developed to allow an XML-based communication between software products that support workflow automation.

BPM

Business Process Management, the discipline of defining, automating and monitoring business processes, usually by means of software tools; also sometimes referred to as Business Process Monitoring, referring to software that monitors business process performance. BPM involves consolidation of data from various sources, querying and analysis of the data, and putting the results into practice. It enhances processes by creating better feedback loops. Continuous and real-time reviews help to identify and eliminate problems before they grow. BPM's forecasting abilities help the company take corrective action in time to meet earnings projections. Forecasting is characterized by a high degree of predictability, which is put to good use to answer 'what-if' scenarios. It is useful in risk analysis and predicting outcomes of merger and acquisition scenarios and coming up with a plan to overcome potential problems. Key performance indicators (KPIs) are provided that help companies monitor efficiency of projects and employees against operational targets. BPM is an acronym in search of a definition . . .

BPMN

Business Process Modeling Notation.

BPR

Business Process Re-engineering, the discipline associated with defining, redesigning and improving business processes and attempting to ignore organizational department constraints/bias.

BRD

Business Requirement Document, the document produced to expressly identify what the business requires an IT system to automate.

COTS

Commercial off-the-shelf Software can be purchased to automate business applications.

CRM

Customer Relationship Management Software, application software that automates customer management.

DCF

Document Co-Formulation, the technique of converting unstructured business knowledge and information, using business document artifacts, and synthesizing this knowledge into a meaningful, coherent framework.

DMAIC

Define Measure Analyze Improve and Control, the phased project framework used by Six Sigma practitioners.

ERP

Enterprise Resource Planning, originally implied application systems designed to plan the utilization of enterprise-wide resources. Although the acronym originated in the manufacturing environment, today's use of the term ERP systems has much broader scope: these systems typically automate all core back-office and internal non-customer facing functions of an organization (finance, human resources, manufacturing, etc.) regardless of the organization's business or charter.

GUI
A graphical user interface is the manner in which humans interface or interact with application software, by means of graphical images in addition to text to represent the information and actions available to the computer/application user.

HIPAA
Health Insurance Portability and Accountability Act, enacted by the US Congress in 1996. The Act protects health insurance coverage for workers and their families when changing or losing their jobs. Title II of HIPAA are the Administrative Simplification (AS) provisions, requiring the establishment of national standards for electronic health care transactions and national identifiers for providers, health insurance plans and employers.

Integrated Computer-Aided Manufacturing (ICAM)
An initiative managed by the USAF at the Wright-Patterson AFB Materials Laboratory, and was part of their Technology Modernization efforts, specifically the Computers in Manufacturing (CIM) initiative.

IDEF
Integrated Definition Languages were initiated by the USAF in the 1970s and developed in the 1980s, covering a range of uses from 'function' modeling to information, simulation, object-oriented analysis and design and knowledge acquisi-

tion. Specifically, a so-called function modeling language. IDEF1X addresses information models, based on entity relationship diagrams.

IT
Information technology, a broad subject concerned with aspects of electronically managing and processing of information.

ITIL®
The Information Technology Infrastructure Library is a framework of 'best practice' approaches intended to facilitate the delivery of high-quality information technology services. It outlines an extensive set of management procedures intended to support businesses in achieving both quality and value for money in IT operations. These procedures are supplier independent and have been developed to provide guidance across the breadth of IT infrastructure, development and operations.

ITOM
Information Technology Operating Model references the broader scope of all IT operating processes and procedures.

KM
Knowledge Management, a range of practices used by organizations to identify, create, represent and distribute knowledge for reuse, awareness and learning across the organization.

MS®
Microsoft Corporation®.

NAM
Nuclear Asset Management Model, a set of 'best practice' process models used to optimally manage nuclear power generation facilities.

NEPA

National Environmental Policy Act, the US environmental law passed January 1, 1970 and President Richard Nixon to protect and preserve the natural environment. Although enacted on January 1, 1970, its 'short title' is National Environmental Policy Act 1969.

NFMA

National Forest Management Act 1976, a US federal law that is the primary statute governing the administration of national forests, and an amendment to the Forest and Rangeland Renewable Resources Planning Act 1974, which called for the management of renewable resources on national forest lands. The 1976 legislation reorganized and expanded the 1974 Act, requiring the Secretary of Agriculture to assess forest lands, and develop and implement a resource management plan for each unit of the National Forest System.

OMG

The Object Management Group is a consortium, originally aimed at setting standards for distributed object-oriented systems, now focuses on modeling (programs, systems and business processes) and model-based standards in some 20 vertical markets. Founded in 1989 by 11 companies (including Hewlett-Packard, IBM, Sun Microsystems, Apple Computer, American Airlines and Data General), it mobilized to create a heterogeneous distributed object standard. The goal was a common portable and inter-operable object model, with methods and data that work using all types of development environments on all types of platforms.

OO

Object-oriented programming paradigm that uses 'objects' to design applications and computer programs. It utilizes several techniques from previously established paradigms, including inheritance, modularity, polymorphism and encapsulation. Even though originated in the 1960s, it was not commonly used in mainstream software application development until the 1990s. Today many popular programming languages (e.g. Java, JavaScript, C#, C++, Python, PHP, Ruby and Objective-C) support OOP. This paradigm has also been hybridized to attempt to model/define 'objects' in the business domain.

PM

Project management is the discipline of organizing and managing resources in such a way that all work required to complete a project within defined scope, time and cost constraints is delivered.

POTS

Plain old telephone service, the standard telephone service that remains the basic form of residential and small-business service nearly everywhere in the world, and the only basic telephone service known to most people until the introduction of the mobile phone. It has been available almost since the introduction of the telephone system in the late 19th century, in a form mostly unchanged to the normal user, despite the introduction of electronic telephone exchanges in the public switched telephone network in the mid-20th century.

QED

Quod erat demonstrandum, the Latin phrase used to indicate that something has been definitively proven.

RBOC

The Regional Bell Operating Companies are the result of the US Department of Justice antitrust suit against the American Telephone & Telegraph Company aka AT&T (not the AT&T Co. created when SBC acquired the old AT&T Co.).

ROI

Return on investment.

SADT

Structured Analysis and Design Technique, a software engineering technique describing systems in a hierarchy of functions.

SCOR

Supply-Chain Operations Reference model, a process reference model developed and endorsed by the Supply-Chain Council as the cross-industry standard diagnostic tool for supply-chain management. SCOR enables users to address, improve and communicate supply-chain management practices within and between all interested parties.

SIPOC

SIPOC considers the *S*uppliers of the process, the *I*nputs to the process, the *P*rocess the team is improving, the *O*utputs of the process and the *C*ustomers that receive the process outputs. The SIPOC diagram is a tool to identify some elements of a process improvement project, helping to define a complex project that may not be well scoped, and typically employed at the measure phase of the Six Sigma DMAIC methodology. Similar and related to process mapping and 'in/out of scope' tools, but provides less detail.

SLA
Service-level agreement.

SME
Subject matter expert is adept in a particular (business) area. Invariably, the term is used when there are professionals with specific business knowledge but without expertise in the field of the application (project) at hand. Sometimes the acronym is voiced ('smee') and other times spelled ('S-M-E').

SNPM
Model for safe, reliable and economically competitive nuclear power generation, and the joint effort of several industry bodies: the Nuclear Energy Institute (NEI), Electric Cost Utility Group and Institute of Nuclear Power Operations (INPO). This model aims to enable benchmarking and improve overall plant performance.

SOA
Service-oriented architecture expresses a perspective of software architecture that defines the use of loosely coupled software services to support the requirements of the business processes and software users. Resources on a network in an SOA environment are made available as independent services that can be accessed without knowledge of their underlying platform implementation or technology.

SOAP

Originally Simple Object Access Protocol, for exchanging XML-based messages over a computer network, normally using HTTP. SOAP forms the foundation layer of the web services stack, providing a basic messaging framework that more abstract layers can build on.

SOX

Sarbanes-Oxley Act 2002 (Pub. L. No. 107-204, 116 Stat. 745), also known as the Public Company Accounting Reform and Investor Protection Act 2002 and commonly called SOX or Sarbox (July 30, 2002), is a US federal law passed in response to a number of major corporate and accounting scandals, including those affecting Enron, Tyco International, Peregrine Systems and WorldCom (recently MCI, and currently now part of Verizon Businesses). The scandals resulted in a decline of public trust in accounting and reporting practices. Named for sponsors Senator Paul Sarbanes (D – Md.) and Representative Michael G. Oxley (R – Oh.), the Act was approved by the House by a vote of 423–3 and by the Senate 99–0. The legislation is wide-ranging and establishes new or enhanced standards for all US public company boards, management and public accounting firms.

Super-SME

Super-subject matter expert is adept in a particular (business) area, with deep expertise in a particular business domain. Invariably, the term is used when there are professionals with specific business knowledge but without expertise in the field of the application (project) at hand. Sometimes the acronym is voiced ('smee') and other times spelled ('S-M-E').

TOGAF

Open Group Architecture Framework for Enterprise Architecture provides a comprehensive approach to the design, planning, implementation and governance of an enterprise information architecture. The architecture is typically modeled at four levels or domains: Business, Application, Data, Technology. A set of foundation architectures is provided to enable the architecture team to envision the current and future state of the architecture.

TQM

Total Quality Management, a philosophy aimed at embedding awareness of quality in all organizational processes. TQM has been widely used in manufacturing, education, government and service industries, as well as NASA space and science programs. It provides an umbrella under which everyone in the organization can strive to improved customer satisfaction.

UML

Unified Modeling Language, a non-proprietary 'specification' language for object modeling. It is a general-purpose modeling language that includes a semi-standardized graphical notation used to create abstract models of systems, referred to as a UML model. It is officially defined at the Object Management Group (OMG) by the UML metamodel – a Meta-Object Facility metamodel (MOF). Like other MOF-based specifications, the UML metamodel and UML models may be serialized in XMI. While UML was designed to specify, visualize, construct and document software-intensive systems, it is not restricted to modeling software. UML is also used for (limited) business process modeling, systems engineering modeling and representing organizational structures. By establishing an industry consensus on a graphic notation to represent common technical concepts like object classes, components, generalization, aggregation and behaviors, it has arguably allowed software developers to concentrate more on design and architecture.

VISIO
Microsoft Visio® is diagramming software for Microsoft Windows®. It uses vector graphics to create diagrams.

VP
Vice-president.

W5
An abbreviation used by xBML practitioners to refer to the five base or foundational dimensions of the xBML framework, namely: What, Who, Where, When and Which.

W5I
An abbreviation used by xBML practitioners to refer to the interrelationships between the five base or foundational dimensions of the xBML framework, namely: What, Who, Where, When and Which.

WfMC
A non-profit organization of adopters, developers, consultants, analysts and university/research groups engaged in Business Process Management (BPM).

xBML

eXtended Business Modeling Language, used to define the business processes of an organization. It is based upon a five-dimensional business framework (What, Who, Where, When and Which) and is uniquely supported by approximately 55 rules that govern the usage, 'output' and 'syntax' of the language. It enables highly consistent, complete and detailed business models to be created, and provides a disciplined methodology to describe a business and its underlying processes. This language is rapidly becoming a standard 'front-end' that many organizations use to define business operations. The output is business-friendly, portable and can be used by many BPM applications.

xBMLi

xBML Innovations, a company that solely produces software tools to support xBML.

XML

Extensible Markup Language, a W3C-recommended general-purpose markup language that supports a wide variety of applications. XML languages or 'dialects' are easy to design and to process, and also designed to be reasonably human-legible. XML is a simplified sub-set of Standard Generalized Markup Language (SGML). Its primary purpose is to facilitate the sharing of data across different information systems, particularly systems connected via the Internet. Formally defined languages based on XML (e.g. RSS, MathML, XHTML, Scalable Vector Graphics, MusicXML and thousands of other examples) allow diverse software reliably to understand information formatted and passed in these languages.

Bibliography

Buzan, T. (2003), *Use Your Head*. BBC Active.

Champy, J. and Hammer, M. (2001), *Reengineering the Corporation: A Manifesto for Business Revolution*. HarperBusiness.

Clark, A.C. (1962), *Profiles of the Future: An Inquiry into the Limits of the Possible*. Harper & Row.

Edwards Deming, W. (2000), *Out of the Crisis*. MIT Press.

Kipling, R. (1987), *The Elephant's Child from Just So Stories*. Scroll Press.

McCoy, D. (2006), Renaissance Man: What's in a name. *Business Integration Journal.*

Moore, G.A. (1998), *Crossing the Chasm: Marketing and Selling High-Tech Products to Mainstream Customers*. Capstone Publishing.

Porter, M. (1998), *Competitive Advantage: Creating and Sustaining Superior Performance*. Free Press.

Senge, P.M. (2004), Creating Desired Futures in a Global Economy. *Reflections: The Society for Organizational Learning Journal*, **5**(1).

Senge, P.M. (1994), *The Fifth Discipline: The Art and Practice of the Learning Organization*. Doubleday.

Smith, A. (1991), *The Wealth of Nations*. Prometheus Books.

Standish Group (1994), *CHAOS Chronicles*. The Standish Group.

Warren, R. (2002), *The Purpose-Driven Life*. Zondervan.

Web references

http://www.BPM.com

http://www.theserverside.com/tt/articles/article.tss?l=BPELJava
http://en.wikipedia.org/wiki/Image:BPMN-E-MailVotingProcess.jpg
http://pigseye.kennesaw.edu/~dbraun/csis4650/A&D/UML_tutorial/
    index.htm
http://syque.com/quality_tools/toolbook/IDEF0/Image24.gif
http://www.lexstudios.com

Index

Note: page numbers in italics refer to figures

Printed in the United States
By Bookmasters